D0438050

SOUTHERN COCKTAILS

SOUTHERN COCKTAILS

DIXIE DRINKS, PARTY POTIONS, AND CLASSIC LIBATIONS

By DENISE GEE | *Photographs by* ROBERT M. PEACOCK

CHRONICLE BOOKS
SAN FRANCISCO

TABLE OF CONTENTS

ACKNOWLEDGMENTS
7

DON'T MIND IF I DO . . .
8

LIKE I WAS SAYIN'
14

Chapter One: **BAR NECESSITIES**
16

RAISING THE BAR: Drink-mixing accessories 17

THE JIG'S UP: A liquor & liqueur checklist 19

IT'S THAT SIMPLE: The must-have simple syrups 22

A GLASS MENAGERIE: What to have on hand—and in hand 23

CURLYCUES: Drink garnishes made simple 23

FLAVOR BOOSTERS: Add zip to your sipper 25

TOAST POINTS: Get-the-party-started sayin's 26

Chapter Two: **THE CLASSICS**
28

CLASSIC MINT JULEP 33

CREOLE BLOODY MARY 34

THE CRUSTA 36

THE HURRICANE 37

FRENCH 75 38

MILK PUNCH 41

ORANGE BLOSSOM 42

PLANTER'S PUNCH 43

PIMM'S CUP 44

RAMOS GIN FIZZ 46

THE SAZERAC 47

THE ROFFIGNAC 49

THE VIEUX CARRÉ 50

TEXT COPYRIGHT © 2007 *by* DENISE GEE.

PHOTOGRAPHS COPYRIGHT
© 2007 *by* ROBERT M. PEACOCK.

ALL RIGHTS RESERVED.
NO PART OF THIS BOOK MAY BE REPRODUCED IN ANY FORM
WITHOUT WRITTEN PERMISSION FROM THE PUBLISHER.

PAGE 117 CONSTITUTES A CONTINUATION OF THE COPYRIGHT PAGE.

LIBRARY OF CONGRESS
CATALOGING-IN-PUBLICATION DATA AVAILABLE.

ISBN-10: 0-8118-5243-1
ISBN-13: 978-0-8118-5243-2

MANUFACTURED IN CHINA

Designed by CATHERINE BULLIMORE

Prop and food styling by DENISE GEE

DISTRIBUTED IN CANADA BY RAINCOAST BOOKS
9050 SHAUGHNESSY STREET, VANCOUVER, BC V6P 6E5

10 9 8 7 6 5 4 3 2 1

CHRONICLE BOOKS LLC
680 SECOND STREET
SAN FRANCISCO, CA 94107

WWW.CHRONICLEBOOKS.COM

Chapter Three: **CHEERS!**
52

APPLE JOUJOU 53

BLUEBERRY MARTINI 54

'BAMA BREEZE 56

COLA HERBSAINT 57

DERBY COOLER 59

GUAVA MAMA 60

HIGH TEA 61

PEACH MOJITO 62

REFINED STRAWBERRY DAIQUIRI 64

SCARLETT O'HARA 65

SEE-THROUGH SANGRÍA 67

THE ULTIMATE MARGARITA 68

WATERMELON CRUSH 71

UPSY-DAISY LEMONADE 72

Chapter Four: **PINKIES UP**
74

CHAMPAGNE PUNCH 75

ABSINTHE FRAPPE 76

THE BEE'S KNEES 79

BLACKBERRY CORDIAL 80

CHIC COSMOPOLITAN 82

MEMPHIS BELLE 83

EUPHORIC EGGNOG 84

FIG PRESERVE MARTINI 87

HERBSAINT CHAMPAGNE COCKTAIL 89

MEYER LEMONTINI 90

SLOE GIN RICKEY 91

MINT JULEP MARTINI 92

PRALINE COFFEE 94

Chapter Five: **NIBBLES**
96

BEER-BATTERED STRING BEANS WITH
RIGHTEOUS RÉMOULADE SAUCE 97

BLACK-EYED PEAS CON QUESO 100

COUNTRY HAM AND GOAT CHEESE PINWHEELS 102

CRAB LOUIS COCKTAIL 103

DEVILISH EGGS 106

FEISTY VIDALIA ONION CHEESE TOASTS 107

FREDDIE LEE'S CHEESE PENNIES 108

SHRIMP IN STOLES WITH DR PEP BBQ SAUCE 111

SPIKED PIMIENTO CHEESE 113

SWEET AND SASSY PECANS 114

EASY DOES IT
116

SOURCES AND PERMISSIONS
117

INDEX
118

TABLE OF EQUIVALENTS
120

DEDICATED TO

All the good people of the Gulf Coast. Onward and upward.

ACKNOWLEDGMENTS

THANK-YOUS TO...

Our dear friend Paige Porter, for thinking of us.

Our editor at Chronicle Books, Bill LeBlond, whose appreciation for Southern storytelling—and the well-made mint julep—led to this project. And cheers as well to Amy Treadwell for her kind guidance on the project; Catherine Bullimore for her designing eye; Rebecca Pepper for her keen editing; and Doug Ogan, Evan Hulka, Brett MacFadden, and Steve Kim for their many contributions.

Dempse and Anne McMullen, for letting us use their beautiful Natchez, Mississippi, home as a prop closet, and Dempse, thanks for your help in styling. And to George and Edith Peacock, for their love—and sweetly putting up with our crazy schedule.

Brenda and Ricky Edgin, whose antebellum home, Rip-Rap, provided a beautiful Natchez backdrop for some of these photos. And their neighbors Doug Mauro and Donald McGlynn, whose hospitality in their historic home and bed-and-breakfast, Oak Hill, was much appreciated. (Especially all that silver polishing!)

Dunleith Plantation in Natchez, for the glorious mint juleps and setting. Sim Callon Jr., for hosting us at the Callon Building. The Center City Grill, for inspiring the photo on page 115. And Leslie Sadler, whose lovely home also served our cause.

Literary agent Angela Miller, for championing our dreams.

Leanne Bailey McMullen, and Susan, Larry, Phillip, Wesley, Mitchell, and Joshua Bellan, for their love and enthusiasm.

The Natchez Historical Society's Ron and Mimi Miller, for their encouragement and guidance. And to the Hotel Monteleone in New Orleans, for being there for us right after Hurricane Katrina.

Designer David Anger and his partner, Jim Broberg, for helping us test
the recipes in style. And to fellow *Better Homes and Gardens* editor Lisa Gaddy
Frederick, for helping keep the creative spark alive.

Sandy Johnson, for sharing her garden—and her friendship.

Charles E. Walton IV, for always helping channel Jean-Anthelme Brillat-Savarin.

Southern Living and *Coastal Living* magazines, for allowing us to experience
wonderful Southern people and traditions.

Chef Scott Peacock of Watershed in Decatur, Georgia, and the late Edna Lewis,
for guiding our Southern foodways conscience.

Lee Bailey, Freddie Lee Bailey, and Freddie Jimerson Bailey in heaven, where we
can still look up to them.

The waiters at every party bar.

DON'T MIND IF I DO...

Someone once asked a group of us Southerners gathered at a cocktail party why
so many storytellers hail from our region.

"There must be something in the water," he figured.

"Yes," I said. "Bourbon."

We're not reared to be alcoholics, mind you, but we are taught how to be
hospitable and have a good time from the get-go. It's what the late, great bon
vivant Eugene Walter—a Mobile native who spent much of his life abroad,
entertaining Southern style—called "dropping the mask": loosening up and
tossing out pretension.

Cocktail hour has been a stressful day's denouement for as long as I
can remember (blame it on the heat—or too much gossip to comprehend in
one day). I discovered this while growing up in my grandmother's house in
Natchez, Mississippi, three hours upriver from New Orleans. (Legend has it
that Natchez was spared during the Civil War when quick-thinking homeowners

buried the silver in the backyard before dolling up to entertain the Union troops. Grant and his men went on to Vicksburg with hangovers, and the rest, as they say, is history.)

Nannie's three-story Victorian manse held the clothing shop Tot & Teen and Mom, antique bric-a-brac and homemade jellies for sale, our living quarters, and a few apartments for rent. Her small galley kitchen overlooked an old carriage house that held her jelly kitchen, which almost always reeked of vinegar (and so did we, since our clothes were laundered there). Needless to say, since so much went on at the corner of Commerce and Orleans Streets, to me and many others, it was the center of the universe.

It was also the center of many a great happy hour. "Is it five o'clock yet?" Nannie would ask, exhausted from batting her eyelashes at the hordes of tourists that would (and still do) flock to Natchez each spring and fall for Pilgrimage home tours. (Natchez has the nation's largest concentration of pre–Civil War houses.) "Yes. Or it is somewhere," my mother, Freddie Lee, the shop's book-keeper, would chime in, and off they'd head to the little spot in the kitchen where various bottles commingled. "It's the witching hour," Nannie would say with glee, fixing herself a bourbon and club soda. I later learned that phrase actually means midnight, but for Nannie and Mama, it was the time for catching up on the day's events with a certain lighthearted cattiness.

Throughout the evenings, neighborhood friends would rotate in and out, many of them charm-braceleted socialites with bulletproof hair and domesticated husbands, others Southern-gothic bohemians obsessed with their complicated lives. Lots of laughter would ensue, as would trays of various tonics—mint juleps, Bloody Marys, and the like—until dinner (always around 9), followed by the slow road to sobriety (sleep). I can still picture a few of those elder statesmen, dressed in pale seersucker suits and bow ties, legs crossed, quietly nodding at their wives' banter.

As I got older and more interested in hearing everyone's stories, I was put in charge of fixing the appetizers Nannie taught me to make: pimiento cheese spread loaded into celery sticks, crabmeat dip for buttery crackers, cheese pennies pulled from a freezer bag and heated in the toaster oven. Quicker nibbles to put out were the spicy pecans we kept sealed in a Mason jar, and sometimes pork rinds, which we gleefully dignified by offering them in a sterling silver bowl.

Like most of the homes I visited, our pantry had more glasses than anyone could imagine or possibly need. There were old-fashioneds, highballs, pilsners, souvenir jiggers, martinis, brandy snifters, Pat O'Brien's hurricane goblets (trophies from the famous Bourbon Street bar), julep cups, and even small jelly jars for serving sherry. An assortment of china platters were on call to serve the edibles. And mismatched linen cocktail napkins stood in for plates (which, truthfully, no one cared to juggle while pursuing their drink).

This anything-goes attitude was even more evident at Natchez's grander parties, of which there were many, since there were many reasons for them—weddings, engagements, debutante announcements, graduations, first communions, promotions, Mardi Gras, Easter, Spring Pilgrimage, and the Kentucky Derby (and those were just the ones during the first five months of the year). Years ago (a little less so now), it was perfectly acceptable to see older children, dressed in their finest, milling about with small cups that got a little bigger every year. At late-afternoon soirees, white-jacketed bartenders would allow us "just a taste, now" of milk punch, mimosas, and mint juleps. Meanwhile, as darkness fell, partygoers would either leave (many without saying a word of good-bye to anyone), be found napping in an upstairs guest bedroom, or glibly announce that they were returning home to brush up on their Bible studies.

We youngsters were knocked off our feet by everyone's lust for life—especially by whoever ate the plastic grapes out of one tabletop's faux-fruit ensemble—but also by our family's trust in us to be responsible in the face of so much temptation. "It's good for you to have a sip or two," my mother reasoned. "It'll keep you from going overboard later."

Fortunately, I've not fallen overboard—there have been day jobs and relationships to consider. And moderation is today's mantra. But there's no doubt that traditional Southern cocktails are officially in my blood, as are many of the newer concoctions I've met along the way. I also love sharing my favorite recipes with friends eager to learn more about the South's culinary heritage. I'm pleased as punch whenever they take their first sip of a mint julep and their eyes light up from the icy, minty, bold sweetness. Afterward, as the famous French epicure Jean-Anthelme Brillat-Savarin so beautifully put it, conversation sparkles. As a dutiful Southerner, I serve the juleps in engraved silver or pewter cups so cold they practically freeze to your hand. I pair them with linen cocktail napkins I've inherited as well as collected over the years—napkins that still serve as "plates" for festive, easy-to-eat appetizers that never fail to have people asking for the particulars.

Nannie and Mama would be proud to know their joie de vivre lives on in these pages.

Now then, that's enough out of me. Is it five o'clock yet?

— Denise Gee

Pat O'Brien's

LIKE I WAS SAYIN'

Some of the best stories stem from an encounter with a cocktail—or three. These legendary Southern natives and transplants say it best.

Tallulah Bankhead told a friend that her doctor had advised her to eat an apple every time she had the urge to drink. She arched an eyebrow and added, "But really, dahlings, sixty apples a day!"
— Tichi Wilkerson, *The Hollywood Reporter,* 1984

Sometimes too much to drink is barely enough.
— Mark Twain (1835–1910)

I stay close to home most of the time—unless, of course, someone's buying dinner, and then I'm a boy with bells on. Otherwise I simply rise and do a bit of sonnet writing, then take a nap, then eat a little, read a little, and then, when there's an emergency—and there most always is—I fill my bathtub up with Jim Beam and swim my way to safety.
— Eugene Walter, to this writer, *Southern Living,* 1998

When one reporter asked if he had any hobbies, [Shelby Foote] replied: "Absolutely not." Then he added, "I drink from time to time."
— Natchez, Mississippi, native Lewis Lord, *U.S. News & World Report,* 2005

What [Papa-Daddy had] really done, he'd drunk another bottle of that prescription. He does it every single Fourth of July as sure as shooting, and it's horribly expensive. Then he falls over in the hammock and snores. So he insisted on zigzagging right on out to the hammock, looking like a half-wit.
— Eudora Welty, *"Why I Live at the P.O.,"* 1941

You're not actually getting anything out of that little cocktail straw, are you?
— Lee Bailey, to this writer, 1989

Well, between Scotch and nothin', I suppose I'd take Scotch. It's the nearest thing to good moonshine I can find.
— William Faulkner, *National Observer,* 1964

A good heavy book holds you down. It's an anchor that keeps you from getting up and having another gin and tonic.
— Roy Blount Jr., "Reading and Nothingness: Of Proust in the Summer Sun," *The New York Times,* June 2, 1985

When you work hard all day with your head and know you must work again the next day, what else can change your ideas and make them run on a different plane like whiskey?
— Ernest Hemingway, *Selected Letters,* 1935

I've been drunk for about a week now, and I thought it might sober me up to sit in a library.
— F. Scott Fitzgerald, *The Great Gatsby,* 1925

Chapter One: BAR NECESSITIES

IF YOU BUILD IT—A PROPER BAR, THAT IS—I CAN ASSURE YOU,
THEY WILL COME.

RAISING THE BAR: Drink Mixing Accessories

To build your bar, find a spot near the dining room and then engage a sturdy accent piece, preferably one with small drawers (or use little baskets to stash your small wares). Here are the basic goods.

BAR SPOON: A long-handled teaspoon works well for stirring and muddling; otherwise, go for the garden-variety twisted-handle type. Just don't use metal ones with carbonated beverages; they can react and turn an unfortunate shade of black.

BLENDER: What better way to soothe a Southern summer than with frozen elixirs? A blender is imperative. Glass canisters are more fun to look through, but stainless-steel ones keep the mix well chilled. Go for one with a powerful motor that doesn't have to scream through getting the work done; powerful ones have lower speeds to get the task accomplished more quietly.

BOTTLE/CAN OPENER: Heirloom ones make conversation pieces.

CITRUS JUICER: Best not to get seeds in your drink, er, mouth.

CITRUS ZESTER/PEELER: Use the zester for fine shreds, the peeler to make quick curls.

COCKTAIL NAPKINS/COASTERS: Cloth ones are more civilized; decorative paper ones are good conversation starters. Avoid plastic coasters—your drinks will slide hither and yon.

COCKTAIL SHAKER: Trust me—buy a good one. The cheap ones will freeze and expand and won't let you remove the strainer lid until a week later. Find one with a lid that's easy to get on and off (but will stay put when you need it to); many even have jigger tops.

CORKSCREW: Otherwise known as a wine bottle opener.

CUTTING BOARD AND PARING KNIFE: So you can work mostly at the bar and not have to traipse back to the kitchen.

DECANTERS: To create a high-style bar, now's the time to ask for your grandparents' glass bottles with those beautiful little "Bourbon," "Gin," "Scotch," and "Vodka" labels hanging round the necks. Or start your own collection after searching antiques shops.

GARNISHES/ACCESSORIES: Be prepared. First impressions are everything. See page 23 for the scoop.

ICE BUCKET/TONGS: Make sure it's beautiful—you don't want one that looks as though it's been lifted from the Sheraton Sarasota. Save those hulky ones for use on a picnic table or boat.

JIGGER: Funny how the more one drinks, the stronger the drinks get. That's because a jigger isn't present. Measure wisely (keep most pours at 1½ ounces) and let the party linger (you don't want to be dragged from the party feet-first). *Note:* 1 jigger equals 1½ ounces, or 3 tablespoons.

LITTLE PARASOLS: Don't use them regularly (you'll get a wince with your martini), but do pull them out when the fun mood or drink strikes.

PITCHER: Not to be confused with "pitchers" of our relatives. Covet ones that have a pinched tip and molded rim that holds back ice.

MALLET: Use only if your refrigerator doesn't offer crushed ice (or someone's getting on your nerves). Otherwise, find a heavy-duty plastic zip-top bag and give your ice a cracking.

MEASURING CUP/SPOONS: I adore my little mixing glass that holds 3 to 4 ounces; seek out sleek measuring spoons that look nice on the bar.

MIXING GLASS: A much more civilized way to make stirred, not shaken, drinks. Find one that's discreetly marked in ounces and cups.

MUDDLER: A utensil for mushing cherries and mashing mint in the mixing glass. You can also use a bar spoon for this.

NOVELTY ICE TRAY: When you want your drinks to make an extra splash.

POUR SPOUTS: If you fear a heavy hand with the bottle, a spout will help you pour with sound mind. It also helps you avoid a sticky mess.

SMALL PLATE FOR COLORED SUGAR/SALT: They're increasingly making "rimmer" containers, so if you can find one of those, good for you.

STIRRERS/SWIZZLE STICKS/PICKS: Use what you've got, but my favorites are vintage hotel bar stirrers and chewable sugarcane sticks. A friend favors chopsticks. Use glass or plastic stirrers, not metal ones, for carbonated beverages—carbonation causes metal stirrers to turn black. Little swords or pronged picks are good for spearing olives, pearl onions, or berries.

STRAINER: It looks formidable, but its purpose is pure: to keep ice out of your glass if you're not using a cocktail shaker and want your beverage straight up.

TOWEL: Clean up your act, but with something that looks presentable.

THE JIG'S UP: A Liquor & Liqueur Checklist

Now, don't rush out and buy all this stuff at once. You'll have a place that looks like my dining room, which, for testing purposes, is brimming with booze (and has visiting repairmen thinking we're quite the swingin' couple). Just build on the basics—gin, bourbon, Scotch, vodka, tequila, and the like (see the Starter Kit, below)—or simply go with your favorites; then begin to experiment with the recipes within this book and stock up on the Next Level (page 20) fare. Most of this stuff will go a long way, especially if you need a dash of this or that, and many are available in trial-size or travel bottles. All will keep for quite awhile if not stored in direct sunlight. For help in ordering some of the harder-to-locate products, refer to the sources on page 117, or check your local spirits distributor or go online.

Note: Jack Daniel's and George Dickel aren't technically bourbons; as Tennessee whiskeys, they're close cousins (for more on that, see the related stories starting on pages 51 and 59). Feel free to use Tennessee whiskey in any recipe calling for bourbon. Pour what you prefer; life is simply interpretive dance anyway.

STARTER KIT

ANGOSTURA BITTERS *1 (4-ounce) bottle*

BEER *Various lagers and/or ales*

CABERNET *1 (750-ml) bottle*

CHAMPAGNE *1 (750-ml) bottle*

CHARDONNAY *1 (750-ml) bottle*

GIN *1 (750-ml) bottle*

GRENADINE *1 (33.8-ounce) bottle*

JACK DANIEL'S TENNESSEE WHISKEY *1 (750-ml) bottle*

KENTUCKY BOURBON *1 (750-ml) bottle*

ORANGE LIQUEUR (COINTREAU *or* **GRAND MARNIER)** *1 (750-ml) bottle*

PEACH SCHNAPPS *1 (750-ml) bottle*

RUM, LIGHT and DARK *1 (750-ml) bottle each*

SCOTCH *1 (750-ml) bottle*

SOUTHERN COMFORT *1 (750-ml) bottle*

TEQUILA *1 (750-ml) bottle*

TRIPLE SEC *1 (750-ml) bottle*

VERMOUTH, DRY and SWEET *1 (750-ml) bottle each*

VODKA *1 (750-ml) bottle*

NEXT LEVEL

APPLE SCHNAPPS *1 (750-ml) bottle*

B&B *or* **BENEDICTINE LIQUEUR**
1 (750-ml) bottle

BLACKBERRY LIQUEUR *1 (750-ml) bottle*

BLUE CURAÇAO *1 (750-ml) bottle*

BRANDY *1 (750-ml) bottle*

CHERRY LIQUEUR *1 (750-ml) bottle*

CITRUS-INFUSED RUM *1 (750-ml) bottle*

CRÈME DE CACAO (CHOCOLATE BEAN)
1 (750-ml) bottle

CRÈME DE CASSIS (CURRANT)
1 (750-ml) bottle

CRÈME DE MENTHE (MINT) *1 (750-ml) bottle*

CRÈME DE NOYAUX (ALMOND)
1 (750-ml) bottle

GEORGE DICKEL TENNESSEE WHISKEY
1 (750-ml) bottle

HERBSAINT, RICARD, *or* **PERNOD (ANISE)**
LIQUEUR *1 (750-ml) bottle*

MINT BITTERS *1 (4-ounce) bottle*

ORANGE BITTERS *1 (12.8-ounce) bottle*

ORANGE FLOWER WATER *1 (8-ounce) bottle*
(or substitute rose water)

PEYCHAUD'S BITTERS *1 (10-ounce) bottle*

PIMM'S NO. 1 LIQUEUR *1 (750-ml) bottle*

PINOT NOIR *1 (750-ml) bottle*

PRALINE LIQUEUR *1 (750-ml) bottle*

RYE WHISKEY *1 (750-ml) bottle*

SAUVIGNON BLANC *1 (750-ml) bottle*

SLOE GIN *1 (750-ml) bottle*

MIXERS, BOTH LEVELS

CLUB SODA

COCKTAIL OLIVES

COLA, DIET and REGULAR

CRANBERRY JUICE

GRAPEFRUIT JUICE

ICED TEA, REFRIGERATED

KOSHER SALT or other "RIMMING" SALT

LEMON-LIME SODA

LEMONADE, REFRIGERATED

LEMONS

LIMES

MARASCHINO CHERRIES with stems

MEYER LEMON SYRUP

ORANGE JUICE

PREPARED HORSERADISH

"RIMMING" SUGAR

ROSE'S LIME JUICE

SIMPLE SYRUP *(page 22)*

SUPERFINE SUGAR

SWEET AND SOUR MIX

TABASCO SAUCE

TOMATO JUICE

TONIC WATER

WORCESTERSHIRE SAUCE

This stuff is liquid gold, and so easy to make. Once you appreciate the beauty of always having it on hand, you'll never go back to mixing sugar (barely) into your drink. Think of giving any or all of the syrups below as a festively bottled gift this holiday season.

SIMPLE SYRUP

1 CUP SUGAR
1 CUP WATER

Combine the sugar and water in a small saucepan. Heat to a boil while stirring. Reduce the heat and continue to stir until the sugar dissolves. Cool to room temperature. Using a funnel, pour the syrup into a clean container and store in the refrigerator indefinitely.

Makes about 1½ cups

MINT SYRUP

Mint fans will love this kicked-up-a-notch simple syrup for making an even mintier julep or for any other cocktail needing more zest.

1 CUP SUGAR
1 CUP WATER
12 FRESH MINT SPRIGS

Combine the sugar and water in a medium saucepan. Heat to a boil while stirring. Reduce the heat and continue to stir until the sugar dissolves. Add the mint and set aside; cool to room temperature. Pour the mint syrup through a strainer into a clean container and store in the refrigerator indefinitely.

Makes about 1½ cups

HONEY SYRUP

1½ CUPS HONEY
½ CUP WATER
¼ CUP FRESHLY SQUEEZED LEMON JUICE
½ TEASPOON GRATED LEMON ZEST

Combine all ingredients in a medium saucepan. Heat to a boil while stirring. Reduce the heat and cook, stirring occasionally, until the mixture is reduced by one-fourth. Set aside until cool. Using a funnel, pour into a clean container and store in the refrigerator for several months.

Makes about 1¾ cups

A GLASS MENAGERIE: What to Have On Hand—and In Hand

When looking for the proper glasses, consider these old reliables. You don't have to have all of these to build your bar—you can improvise with most anything—but here are the basics.

Champagne flute, 6 to 8 ounces
Collins glass, 10 to 12 ounces
Cordial, 2 to 4 ounces
Demitasse/espresso cup, 3 ounces
Highball glass, 8 to 10 ounces
Irish coffee mug, 8 ounces
Martini glass, 4 to 6 ounces
Old-fashioned (or "rocks") glass, 8 to 10 ounces
Pilsner glass, 12 to 14 ounces
Shot glass, 2 ounces
Small old-fashioned glass, 4 ounces
Sour glass, 6 ounces
Wine goblets (separate ones for white and red wines), 10 to 14 ounces

CURLYCUES: Drink Garnishes Made Simple

I'm a sucker for a well-dressed drink—and so is most everyone else. Lemon wedges are fine, but they don't win any beauty pageants when it comes to showing your party guests how much you care. Not all of these are curly, but they'll definitely add bling. When making them, use a paring knife for accuracy. Store your creations in a sealed bowl or airtight bag until ready for use.

CITRUS CURLS *(for anything in a martini glass)*
Use your vegetable peeler (or better yet, the small-peel slot on a quality zester) to cut a citrus peel into a thin ¼-inch-wide spiral, rotating the utensil around the peel. Once you've gone two turns or so around the fruit, taper off the spiral to complete the twist. Continue doing this with the rest of the peel. If desired, curl the end around a straw or pencil and refrigerate or briefly freeze until needed.

CITRUS KNOTS *(for martinis and the like)*
Take long, thin curls or strips of citrus peel and carefully tie each into a knot.

CITRUS TWISTS *(for classic cocktails)*
Cut ⅛-inch-thick slices from the fruit. Cut halfway across each slice, stopping at the center (so as not to cut into the bitter pith), and twist the ends in opposite directions to release the oils into the drink. With short twists, you can either drop the peel into the drink or let it sit daintily on the lip of the glass. For long twists, drop one end into the drink and dangle the other on the rim of the glass.

CITRUS WEDGES *(for old-fashioned cocktails)*
Think of cutting an orange to eat: Using a sharp knife, cut off each end of the fruit. Cut in half lengthwise into two sections. With the rind side down, make one cut lengthwise down to, but not through, the rind. Turn over and slice into ¼- to ½-inch wedges.

CITRUS OR VEGGIE WHEELS *(for tropical or Bloody Mary drinks)*
Cut a ¼-inch diagonal slice of a fruit or vegetable (think pineapple or cucumber) and make a cut at one end, leaving the skin intact. Affix to the edge of the glass.

CUCUMBER PLANK *(for Pimm's Cups)*
Slice an English (seedless) cucumber and cut into thin 4-inch lengths to use as stirrers.

DRESSY FRUIT *(for tropical drinks)*
Star fruit (carambola) slices (gold means ripe); kiwi slices (cut in half, gently scoop out of the fuzzy skin, and slice); partially sliced strawberries (hulls attached); cut peaches or apples; julienned apple "matchsticks" (with peel intact at the top). When making in advance, store these delicate fruits in a lemon-lime beverage in the refrigerator to prevent browning.

EDIBLE FLOWERS *(for more delicate drinks, champagne, reception or brunch punch)*
Ooh la la. Just nibble them before the drink does.

GREEN ONION FIRECRACKERS *(for Bloody Marys or margaritas)*
Cut the root ends and most of the top parts from green onions. Make several cuts on the green ends to create what looks like fringe. Immerse them in ice water and the ends will curl up.

VEGGIE KABOBS *(for Bloody Marys)*
Skewer the desired mix of cucumber slices, celery portions, radishes, small okra, baby corn, olives (black and green), and fresh butter (lima) beans.

VEGGIE STIRRERS *(for Bloody Marys)*
Think green beans, vertical carrot slices, pickled okra, and fresh celery (leaves attached).

FLAVOR BOOSTERS: Add Zip To Your Sipper

Live a little—more—with added cocktail oomph.

ANGOSTURA BITTERS: Clovey, orangey drops of goodness.

CINNAMON STICK

CITRUS TWISTS

FROZEN MELON BALLS AS "ICE"

GINGER, sliced thin and vertically as a stirrer.

MARASCHINO CHERRIES: Now available in a variety of colors and flavors.

MINT AND MORE MINT!

OLIVES (black and green), preferably pimiento-stuffed.

PEYCHAUD'S BITTERS: Reminiscent of cherry cough syrup.

POWDERED SUGAR: Many like it atop mint juleps and daiquiris.

SALT RIM: Rub a lime or lemon wedge around the glass edge to moisten it. Spread coarse salt evenly on a small plate. Turn the glass over and gently twist to distribute the salt evenly around the rim.

SAUCES/SEASONINGS: Worcestershire, Tabasco, Cajun.

SIMPLE (SUGAR) SYRUPS: Just as they always keep a ham in the fridge, good Southerners keep some sugar syrup on hand to avoid having to stir like crazy for it to dissolve. See page 22.

SUGAR RIM: Rub the rim of a glass with a slice of citrus; dip the edge of the rim into a small bowl of superfine sugar (don't use granulated unless you like the feeling of sand on your lips).

SUGARCANE SKEWERS/STIRRERS

SWEET TOPPERS: Coconut flakes, chocolate, nutmeg, cinnamon.

WHIPPED CREAM: Okay, I'll admit it—I'm the one who doesn't like marshmallows on my sweet potato casserole or whipped cream on my daiquiri. If you're game to look like a tourist in my book, go for it. I'll just be ribbing you.

TOAST POINTS: Get-The-Party-Started Sayin's

Toasting dates back to the South—of England. Purportedly, in Bath, in 1709, a young man became smitten with a young woman enjoying one of the Roman-era baths. He cupped his hands, drank a bit of the water she was relaxing in, and professed his love for her. Whereupon a wisecracking competing suitor countered that he never drank in the morning. Instead, he preferred to savor the toast being dipped in the warm liquor.

As for clinking our glasses, the story goes that Vikings rammed their cups together so that liquid would flow from cup to cup, thus ensuring that it was safe to drink (poisoning was rampant).

Anyhoo, some toasts worth memorizing and repeating:

To health and prosperity for our enemies' enemies.
— Welsh proverb

Let us toast the fools; but for them, the rest of us could not exceed.
— Mark Twain

In matters of style, swim with the currents. In matters of principle, stand like a rock.
— Thomas Jefferson

He who drinks gets drunk.
He who gets drunk falls to sleep.
He who sleeps does not sin.
He who doesn't sin goes to heaven.
So let's all drink and go to heaven!
— Irish proverb that hung over my grandparents' bar

While we live, let us live.
— Anonymous

Cool breeze, cozy fire, full moon, easy chairs, empty plates, tall tales, sweet songs, soft words, short sips, long life.
— John Egerton

Failure is the condiment that gives success its flavor.
— Truman Capote

Here's to us all! God bless us every one!
— Tiny Tim's toast in *A Christmas Carol* by Charles Dickens

May you always have red-eye gravy with your ham, hush puppies with your catfish, and the good sense not to argue with your wife.
— Timothy Noah, "A Tennessee Toast," *The New Republic*

Up to my lips and down to my hips
The further it goes, the better it gits.
Here's to peace at home and plenty abroad.
Love your wife and serve the Lord—Drink!
— Early antebellum South toast

May you be surrounded by good food, even better wine, and loved ones this and every month of the year.
— Donna Florio

Chapter Two: THE CLASSICS

TRADITIONS KEEP THE FABRIC OF THE SOUTH RICHLY WOVEN, AND THE
REGION'S TRIED-AND-TRUE COCKTAILS ARE DECIDEDLY ITS LIQUID ASSETS.

Never has a recipe, especially for a beverage, been so eloquent. Consider this letter from then–Lieutenant General (later General) Simon Bolivar Buckner Jr., the son of General Simon Bolivar Buckner of the Confederate Army, who lost Fort Donelson to General Ulysses S. Grant. Here, in a letter dated March 30, 1937, Buckner writes to Major General William D. Connor, superintendent of the U.S. Military Academy at West Point.

My dear General Connor,

Your letter requesting my formula for mixing mint juleps leaves me in the same position in which Captain Barber found himself when asked how he was able to carve the image of an elephant from a block of wood. He replied that it was a simple process consisting merely of whittling off the part that didn't look like an elephant. The preparation of the quintessence of gentlemanly beverages can be described only in like terms.

A mint julep is not the product of a formula. It is a ceremony and must be performed by a gentleman possessing a true sense of the artistic, a deep reverence for the ingredients, and a proper appreciation of the occasion. It is a rite that must not be entrusted to a novice, a statistician, nor a Yankee. It is a heritage of the old South, an emblem of hospitality, and a vehicle in which noble minds can travel together upon the flower-strewn paths of happy and congenial thought.

So far as the mechanics of the operation are concerned... Go to a spring where cool, crystal-clear water bubbles from under a bank of dew-washed ferns. In a consecrated vessel, dip up a little water at the source. Follow the stream through its banks of green moss and wild-flowers until it broadens and trickles through beds of mint growing in aromatic profusion and waving softly in the summer breezes.

Gather the sweetest and tenderest shoots and gently carry them home. Go to the sideboard and select a decanter of Kentucky Bourbon, distilled by a master hand, mellowed with age yet still vigorous and inspiring. An ancestral sugar bowl, a row of silver goblets, some spoons, and some ice and you are ready to start. In a canvas bag, pound twice as much ice as you think you will need. Make it fine as snow, keep it dry, and do not allow it to degenerate into slush.

In each goblet, put a slightly heaping teaspoonful of granulated sugar, barely cover this with spring water. Slightly bruise one mint leaf into this, leaving the spoon in the goblet. Then pour elixir from the decanter until the goblets are about one-fourth full. Fill the goblets with snowy ice, sprinkling in a small amount of sugar as you fill. Wipe the outsides of the goblets dry, and embellish copiously with mint.

Then comes the important and delicate operation of frosting. By proper manipulation of the spoon, the ingredients are circulated and blended until Nature, wishing to take a further hand and add another of its beautiful phenomena, encrusts the whole in a glittering coat of white frost. Thus harmoniously blended by the deft touches of a skilled hand, you have a beverage eminently appropriate for honorable men and beautiful women.

When all is ready, assemble your guests on the porch or in the garden, where the aroma of the juleps will rise Heavenward and make the birds sing. Propose a worthy toast, raise the goblet to your lips, bury your nose in the mint, inhale a deep breath of its fragrance, and sip the nectar of the gods.

Being overcome by thirst, I can write no further.

Sincerely,

S. B. Buckner Jr.

BLUE(GRASS) VELVET

Like jazz, bourbon is truly American. Its birth dates to 1791, when the Distilled Spirits Tax led to the Whiskey Rebellion, and angry Scotch-Irish moonshiners (who'd made Scotch from barley in their native Scotland and Ireland) headed west to the region now known as Kentucky. The thing is, barley didn't grow well there, so the 'shiners planted rye instead, which German settlers had been using to make schnapps. Somehow or other, distilling corn became interesting, especially in Kentucky, where the fertile bottom loam of limestone-water creeks helped raise richly flavored grain.

Bourbon as we know it originates with the Reverend Elijah Craig, who hailed from Kentucky's Bourbon County (so named for the French, who helped the region during the Revolutionary War). The frugal distiller was unique in that he used old, charred oak barrels to transport his whiskey to New Orleans. As an unexpected plus, the "Bourbon" whiskey mellowed during the journey, becoming a rich caramel color. And it was very much admired.

In 1964, the term "bourbon" was protected by a congressional resolution mandating that it must be distilled under 160 proof; be a minimum of two years old; be made from a mash of at least 51 percent corn; have nothing added at bottling to enhance sweetness, color, or flavor; and be aged in charred new oak barrels.

Premium-bourbon makers vary in their philosophy and methodology. Some distill and age their bourbon at a different proof, others pay closer attention to barrel rotation. Sometimes the corn is cracked beforehand, other times it's rolled. Here are its leading classifications.

Single-barrel: These result from the bottling of one single barrel of bourbon, which has been tested to see if it's the cream of the crop and aged to perfection much longer than the average bourbon. The first to offer this style was Leestown Distilling (formerly Ancient Age), which put Blanton's on the market in 1984. Others that followed include Elijah Craig 18 Years Old, Elmer T. Lee Single Barrel, Henry McKenna Single Barrel, and Evan Williams Single Barrel Vintage.

Small-batch: Originating from a mixed batch of bourbons, this style is the brainchild of the Jim Beam Distillery, which had the philosophy that single barrels are too unpredictable to bottle individually. To provide more uniformity, their thought was to combine the very best barrels to make small batches featuring the best of grain formulas, bottling proofs, filtering processes, and ages. Other well-known small-batch bourbons include Baker's, Booker's, Basil Hayden's, Knob Creek, Maker's Mark, and Woodford Reserve.

Small-scale: This is where Maker's Mark makes its mark—as a "micro-distillery," making only about 54 barrels of bourbon a day. (It also is notable for using wheat, which yields a "softer" bourbon than rye.) Because it has more time to cultivate each barrel, Maker's Mark can cook the mash slowly. It also uses well-seasoned cypress barrels and an all-copper still, and rotates its barrels in a well-honed, time-honored tradition.

The Kentucky Bourbon Festival features special bourbon events and tastings the third weekend of September; call (800) 638-4877 or visit www.kybourbonfestival.com.

To learn more about Kentucky's bourbon country and related distillery tours, go online to www.kybourbon.com and www.straightbourbon.com.

CLASSIC MINT JULEP

There are many variations of this beloved drink—Commander's Palace in New Orleans adds ¼ ounce of brandy to theirs—but this is the classic I adore. Juleps are best made one by one for true artisanal beauty, and are meant to be sipped from crushed ice, never cubed. Friendly debates go on about using simple syrup versus plain water and sugar, or using regular sugar instead of fine or powdered, but simple syrup has the two more smoothly blended. If you don't have simple syrup on hand, substitute 1 tablespoon cold water and 1 teaspoon superfine sugar. Just don't wait for the Kentucky Derby to enjoy it.

6 OR 7 FRESH MINT LEAVES

1 TABLESPOON SIMPLE SYRUP *(page 22)*

2 OUNCES BOURBON

Garnish: **MINT SPRIG**

Combine the mint leaves, syrup, and bourbon in a silver julep cup or cocktail glass. Using a bar spoon, crush the mint to release its essence into the liquid. Fill the cup with crushed ice. Gently press the spoon into the ice, shaking it to incorporate the bourbon-syrup mixture. Add the garnish.

Serves 1

CREOLE BLOODY MARY

This recipe is adapted from the popular drink at the Under-the-Hill Saloon in Natchez, Mississippi—a 200-year-old riverside establishment legendary for its colorful history of serving gamblers and floozies. Nowadays, longtime bartender J. D. Montgomery—standing just a head above bar height—fills tall orders for this zesty drink, which is almost always made to the tune of blaring rhythm and blues. Outside the joint, mammoth rocking chairs await your presence on cool evenings, where you can kick back and watch the Mississippi River glide past.

6 CUPS TOMATO JUICE

2 CUPS VODKA

¾ CUP FRESHLY SQUEEZED LEMON JUICE

4 TABLESPOONS PREPARED HORSERADISH

2 TABLESPOONS WORCESTERSHIRE SAUCE

1 TABLESPOON HOT SAUCE

1 TABLESPOON CREOLE SEASONING

1 TEASPOON FRESHLY GROUND BLACK PEPPER

½ TEASPOON CAYENNE PEPPER

Garnishes: **PICKLED OKRA POD, LONG GREEN BEAN, OR CARROT STICK**

Add all ingredients except the garnish to a pitcher. Stir well, and chill until needed.

Pour the mixture into 8 wide-mouth glasses filled with ice. Sprinkle with extra Creole seasoning, and garnish as desired.

Serves 8

THE CRUSTA

Legend has it that this refined, amber-colored beauty was invented in New Orleans at an unrefined-sounding place called Santini's Saloon, probably in the mid-nineteenth century. But who knows for sure about any story handed down over the decades—especially if this beverage has been enjoyed while the story unfolded. The cognac gives it a mellowness and the bourbon more of an edge. In a pinch you can use maraschino cherry juice instead of the liqueur, but you'll get a much sweeter drink.

1 TABLESPOON SUPERFINE SUGAR

1 LEMON WEDGE

1½ OUNCES COGNAC OR BOURBON

½ OUNCE ORANGE LIQUEUR

1½ TEASPOONS MARASCHINO CHERRY LIQUEUR

½ OUNCE FRESHLY SQUEEZED LEMON JUICE

DASH OF ANGOSTURA BITTERS

Garnish: ORANGE CURL

Place the sugar in a shallow bowl. Rub the rim of a wineglass with the lemon wedge and dip it into the sugar; discard the lemon.

Fill the glass with crushed ice.

Combine the cognac, liqueurs, lemon juice, and bitters in a cocktail shaker filled with ice. Shake and strain into the glass. Add the garnish.

Serves 1

THE HURRICANE

This is decidedly a group drink, preferably served by the green-jacketed waiters at New Orleans's Pat O'Brien's, longtime stomping grounds for my family (especially the piano bar room). Supposedly, the bar began as a speakeasy called Mr. O'Brien's Club Tipperary, where the password to get in was "storm's brewin'." The place thrived secretly, not far from its current location. Fortunately, Prohibition ended, but one of the most popular punches served there didn't. Here's a make-at-home version that comes pretty close to the real thing.

1½ CUPS PINEAPPLE JUICE

1¼ CUPS FRESHLY SQUEEZED ORANGE JUICE

1 CUP FILTERED (NOT CLOUDY) POMEGRANATE JUICE

½ CUP GRENADINE

½ CUP SIMPLE SYRUP *(page 22)*

½ CUP FRESHLY SQUEEZED LIME OR LEMON JUICE,
PLUS MORE TO TASTE

1¼ CUPS LIGHT RUM

1½ OUNCES DARK RUM

2 OUNCES TRIPLE SEC

Garnishes: ORANGE AND LEMON SLICES,
MARASCHINO CHERRIES WITH STEMS

Combine all ingredients except for the garnishes in a large pitcher and stir well. Serve in 16-ounce glasses over lots of cubed ice, adorned with the trio of garnishes.

Serves about 6

FRENCH 75

This cocktail pays homage to France's two powerful weapons—guns and champagne. The French 75mm field gun was a hit overseas during World War I, with American soldiers returning home to praise the small cannon's success in battle. By around 1920, a drink with the same name began to surface in New Orleans's French Quarter. You'll find this to be a sublimely elegant summer drink, especially when served in vintage champagne glasses. (Shown here are Historic Natchez Collection reproductions of antique flutes from the antebellum home Mistletoe.) Many prefer the more pert gin version, but others like the drink sweeter, and use brandy instead.

2 OUNCES GIN OR BRANDY
½ CUP FRESHLY SQUEEZED LEMON JUICE
3 TABLESPOONS SIMPLE SYRUP *(page 22)*
⅔ CUP DRY CHAMPAGNE, CHILLED
Garnish: **LEMON OR ORANGE CURL** *(optional)*

Put the gin, lemon juice, and syrup in a cocktail shaker. Add ice cubes and shake vigorously.

Strain the mixture into 2 champagne flutes. Add the champagne and garnish (if using) just before serving.

Serves 2

MILK PUNCH

Much like the mighty mint julep, this drink is de rigueur for any daytime soiree in the South, where it's typically served in a sterling silver punch bowl. Its creamy persuasion lies in its bold bourbon balanced with sweet vanilla. Milk punch always makes a splash at a brunch or daytime wedding, but it's also nice during the fall holidays, as a pre-dessert sipper in lieu of eggnog. It should be served very cold.

3 QUARTS HALF-AND-HALF
1 BOTTLE *(750-ml)* **BOURBON OR BRANDY**
¼ CUP PURE MEXICAN VANILLA OR VANILLA EXTRACT
2 CUPS POWDERED SUGAR
Garnish: **GRATED NUTMEG**

Combine all ingredients except the nutmeg in a gallon-size container. Cover and freeze until the mixture is slightly frozen.

Use an ice pick to make the mixture slightly slushy. Pour into a punch bowl or chilled pitcher. Add more powdered sugar, if desired. Sprinkle with nutmeg.

Pour into small cocktail glasses or wine goblets (not over ice). Garnish each drink with an additional pinch of nutmeg.

Serves 16 to 20

ORANGE BLOSSOM

I've never been a fan of such orange juice–based cocktails as the screwdriver (orange juice and vodka); somehow the harshness of the juice can take on a metallic edge with the liquor. This, however, is an exception. Sporting a smooth gin, the drink has just the right amount of orange juice to give it color and fragrance, and a bit of lime juice as a nod to its south Florida origins. The beverage was reportedly developed when the Sunshine State made the orange blossom its official flower in 1909.

1½ OUNCES GIN
1 OUNCE FRESHLY SQUEEZED ORANGE JUICE
½ OUNCE FRESHLY SQUEEZED LIME JUICE
½ OUNCE SIMPLE SYRUP *(page 22)*
Garnish: ORANGE OR LIME TWIST

Combine all ingredients except the garnish in a cocktail shaker filled with ice; shake well to combine. Strain into a chilled martini glass and add the garnish.

Serves 1

PLANTER'S PUNCH

This deeply tropical drink hails from Cuba, where, on balmy days, sugarcane magnates might've cooled off with it after lording over their minions (who themselves no doubt needed a drink). Typically, this cocktail is made with 2 parts orange juice to 1 part pineapple juice. Lemonade makes a sprightly substitute for the pineapple juice, plus it keeps the mix icy and adds a distinctive hue.

1 *(750-ml)* BOTTLE DARK RUM

1 *(6-ounce)* CAN FROZEN PINK LEMONADE CONCENTRATE

1 *(6-ounce)* CAN FROZEN ORANGE JUICE CONCENTRATE

2 OUNCES FRESHLY SQUEEZED LIME JUICE

1½ OUNCES GRENADINE

4 CUPS WATER

Garnishes: ORANGE SLICE AND MARASCHINO CHERRY

Combine all ingredients except the garnishes in a large container; stir well.

Chill until ready to serve, then ladle or pour into punch cups or ice-filled cocktail glasses. Add the garnishes.

Serves 14 to 16

PIMM'S CUP

This drink—which my friend Pableaux Johnson calls "a well-tanned Tom Collins"—closely follows the Pimm's Cup cocktail served at the historic Napoleon House in New Orleans, a dark, moody, and delicious place to be on a late afternoon. Created in 1840 in England, the Pimm's recipe is a closely guarded secret. We know that 7 Up, which the Napoleon House uses, wasn't the accompaniment of choice back then, but we imagine it was added decades ago to help counteract the South's high humidity. You'll enjoy the spicy, herbaceous finish of the amber, gin-based liqueur. A cucumber slice adds the perfect touch of freshness.

1¼ OUNCES PIMM'S NO. 1 LIQUEUR

4 OUNCES LEMONADE

1 OUNCE 7UP

Garnish: CUCUMBER SLICE

Pour the liqueur, lemonade, and 7 Up into a highball glass filled with ice; stir well. Add the garnish.

Serves 1

RAMOS GIN FIZZ

The Gin Fizz slips on like a fine linen suit. It has been a darling of socialites since the 1880s, when it was developed by New Orleanian Henry C. Ramos. Notorious Louisiana Governor Huey P. Long knew its charms well, reportedly hiring New Orleans's Roosevelt Hotel bartender to accompany him to New York so he could enjoy this white, creamy, floral but tart gin fizz at a moment's notice.

2 OUNCES GIN

1 OUNCE FRESHLY SQUEEZED LEMON JUICE

1 EGG WHITE

1 OUNCE SIMPLE SYRUP *(page 22)*

1 OUNCE ORANGE FLOWER OR ROSE WATER

1 OUNCE HALF-AND-HALF

CLUB SODA

Garnish: **ORANGE WHEEL**

Pour the gin, lemon juice, egg white, syrup, orange flower water, and half-and-half into a cocktail shaker filled with a few ice cubes; shake for about a minute. Strain into a pilsner glass or tall, slim glass filled with ice; top with club soda and stir. Add the garnish.

Serves 1

THE SAZERAC

This is the true New Orleans insider's drink, created in some form or another in the early 1800s by the Creole apothecary Antoine Amadie Peychaud. The founding father of Peychaud's bitters hailed from the West Indies and had a drugstore on Royal Street in New Orleans called Pharmacie Peychaud. He served this beverage, actually a stomach tonic that included absinthe, in a *coquetier* (egg cup)—the word that supposedly evolved into "cocktail." (And the vessel that served as inspiration for the jigger.) Down the street from Peychaud was the Sazerac Coffee House (also a bar), which promoted the drink but soon added a French cognac. In 1949, the Sazerac bar relocated to the Roosevelt Hotel (now the Fairmont Hotel), where you can still savor old New Orleans. This drink is like spun honey—golden, with a time-honored depth thanks to the rye. I particularly like using Old Overholt rye, with its hints of honey and spice.

⅛ TEASPOON HERBSAINT OR PERNOD LIQUEUR

2 OUNCES RYE WHISKEY OR SMALL-BATCH BOURBON

1 TEASPOON SIMPLE SYRUP *(page 22; see Note)*

3 OR 4 DASHES PEYCHAUD'S BITTERS

1 STRIP LEMON PEEL

Pour the liqueur into a small, chilled old-fashioned glass and swirl it along the sides of the glass before discarding the excess liquid, if desired.

Combine the rye, simple syrup, and bitters in a cocktail shaker filled with ice; shake well to combine.

Moisten the edge of the glass with the lemon peel. Strain the cocktail into the glass, and drop in the peel.

Serves 1

Note: Though not traditional, I love substituting Meyer lemon syrup. See the sources on page 117 if you can't find it locally.

THE ROFFIGNAC

Here's one inspired by a drink popular in the days of Count Louis Philippe Joseph de Roffignac, mayor of New Orleans during the early 1820s. Life was much better for the count then, since he'd successfully made a hasty retreat from France to the French Quarter in 1800 to escape the guillotine. Roffignac reportedly settled into a house on Chartres Street between Dumaine and St. Philippe Streets, and did much to beautify the growing city. It's there that he no doubt enjoyed the drink that's now attributed to him, having been passed down for almost two centuries via word of mouth and hand of bartender. It comes on strong but finishes sweet.

2 OUNCES COGNAC OR RYE WHISKEY
1 OUNCE RASPBERRY SYRUP *(see Note)*
CLUB SODA
Garnish: **FRESH RASPBERRIES**

Pour the cognac and raspberry syrup into a stemmed cocktail glass filled with ice. Top it off with club soda, and swizzle to blend. Add the garnish.

Serves 1

Note: Raspberry syrup can be found in most gourmet coffee and tea shops.

THE VIEUX CARRÉ

This is a strong drink. A manly-man drink. And it's the pride of the Hotel Monteleone in New Orleans's French Quarter, or "old square" (hence "Vieux Carré"), where former bartender Walter Bergeron is known to have developed it in the late 1930s. Just like the historic hotel's Italianate carousel bar, this drink can get a bit dizzying after a while, so savor it slowly, friends.

1 OUNCE RYE WHISKEY OR BOURBON

1 OUNCE COGNAC

1½ OUNCES SWEET VERMOUTH

1 TEASPOON BENEDICTINE LIQUEUR

DASH PEYCHAUD'S BITTERS

DASH ANGOSTURA BITTERS

Pour all of the ingredients into a cocktail glass filled with ice; stir well.

Serves 1

YOU DON'T KNOW JACK (UNTIL NOW)

For many, "Jack and Coke" means "bourbon and Coke." Truth is, Jack Daniel's isn't a bourbon at all. It's a Tennessee whiskey, known for a unique charcoal filtering technique that leaves it rich, sweet, and a little spicy. The filtering is an added step that bourbon doesn't get; otherwise, they're pretty much created in the same way, making them distant cousins—but not brothers.

Speaking of brothers, and sisters too, the whiskey's namesake, Jack Daniel, had them—12 of 'em. Because of the economic hardships of his large family in early Tennessee, little Jasper Newton "Jack" Daniel was raised by a family friend six years after his birth in 1850. It wasn't long before he was hired by a Lutheran minister to help run a burgeoning whiskey still on Tennessee's intriguingly named Louse River. And by the ripe old age of 13, Jack was handed the keys to the still—and his future—when the minister decided to focus on the Holy Spirit instead of the holding spirit.

There in the village of Lynchburg, young master Jack went on to perfect the still's secret weapon: mellowing fresh whiskey through hard maple charcoal, which made it a premium-tasting whiskey—and a bit more expensive. Such commitment to greatness tested Jack's commitment to the bottom-line, especially during the Civil War, but he stuck to his guns, registering his distillery a year after the war ended. That makes it the oldest registered distillery in the United States. Its square bottle, too, is distinctive. It was created in 1895 (replacing its jug predecessor) in order for Jack Daniel's Old No. 7 Brand Tennessee Whiskey (80 proof) to stand out.

Tragically, Jack's life took a turn downward in 1905, when, having forgotten the combination to his office safe, he kicked it in anger, breaking his toe. An infection set in that plagued him for six years, eventually hastening his death. Since Jack wasn't married and didn't have any children, the distillery went into the hands of one of his sidekicks, nephew Lem Motlow, who guided it through Prohibition.

Happily, Jack's finely tuned flavor lives on in deep amber bliss—aromatically woodsy, smooth, and easily sippable, with hints of spice and caramel. It all stems from having the fresh whiskey—made from corn, rye, barley malt, and iron-free water from a limestone-cave spring—slowly drip through gargantuan containers hard-packed with 10 feet of sugar maple charcoal. During the 10-day process, the whiskey absorbs the smoky charcoal's essence, which is amplified by the charred oak barrels it ages in for four years.

Of course, like its bourbon compadres, Tennessee whiskey has also reached the top shelf of fine bars. A case in point is Jack Daniel's Single Barrel Tennessee Whiskey (94 proof)—hand-crafted, tested for superiority, and aged in charred white oak barrels in the upper floors of select warehouses for three years longer than its flagship spirit, making it more mature and robust. For those with milder palates, there's Gentleman Jack (80 proof), charcoal-mellowed a second time for a lighter, cognac-like whiskey. And if you see Jack Daniel's with a green label (80 proof), that means it's been aged elsewhere in the warehouse to create a slightly lighter-colored, more delicate version of its black-labeled brother.

Back to some did-you-know fun: Jack Daniel's is made in a dry county, which presumably forces the 361 residents to drive to the next county to buy their own county's lifeblood. Check out the free distillery tour the next time you're near Nashville (Lynchburg is 70 miles to the southeast), or go online to www.jackdaniels.com.

Chapter Three: # CHEERS!

SOUTHERNERS NEVER NEED MUCH REASON TO PARTY, BUT THESE FESTIVE
DRINKS ARE CERTAINLY GOOD STARTS.

APPLE JOUJOU

You hear the word *joujou* a lot in the Southern port cities of New Orleans, Mobile, and Charleston. It sounds like both the French term for "plaything" and the African word for "sacred object." Both meanings are fitting for this smooth and golden drink. Imbibing it will have you possessive of your glass in no time. The playfulness here is the wonderful flavor of apple, which makes for the best apple "juice" ever.

2 OUNCES APPLE SCHNAPPS

½ CUP LEMONADE

2 OUNCES SOUTHERN COMFORT

Garnish: **GREEN OR RED APPLE SLIVERS**

Pour all ingredients except the garnish into a cocktail shaker filled with ice; mix well.

Strain into 2 old-fashioned cocktail glasses filled with ice. Add the garnish.

Serves 2

SOUTHERN COMFORT ZONE

Southern Comfort, in its original form as Cuffs & Buttons, was created in New Orleans in 1874 by M. W. Heron in his bar near Bourbon Street. Heron made the caramel-hued spirit from bourbon and marinated peaches, serving it from a whiskey barrel. To introduce his creation to even more people, he moved his act upriver to Memphis, and by 1889 began selling bottles of his peach-flavored bourbon-based liqueur for $2.50, signing each one personally. He then moved even farther upriver to St. Louis, where his potion won a gold medal at the 1904 World's Fair. In 1934, the spirit was renamed Southern Comfort and took on a new label featuring a Currier & Ives print of the Mississippi plantation Woodland (now a bed-and-breakfast inn). The company made another splash four years later when it created the Scarlett O'Hara drink (page 65) in honor of *Gone With the Wind*. Southern Comfort is now based in Louisville, Kentucky; for more information, go to www.southerncomfort.com.

BLUEBERRY MARTINI

Berries are the gems of childhood. For me, they evoke memories of U-pick farms, or of squirreling away a few stray ones to nibble on while Nannie made fried berry pies. I'm sure that's why berry drinks bring out the kid in us all—as they do for cousins Pearce and Ann Bailey, who own and operate Bailey's Berry Patch outside of Dallas (and shared this recipe with me).

HANDFUL OF FRESH, WASHED BLUEBERRIES *(about 20 small)*
1½ OUNCES VODKA
½ OUNCE BLUE CURAÇAO LIQUEUR
⅓ OUNCE FRESHLY SQUEEZED LEMON JUICE, OR MORE TO TASTE
Garnish: **SEVERAL BERRIES SKEWERED ON A COCKTAIL PICK**

Muddle the blueberries in a cocktail shaker. Add the vodka, curaçao, and lemon juice. Fill the shaker with ice. Shake vigorously to help the blueberries release more color and flavor. Strain through a fine-mesh sieve into a chilled martini glass. Add the garnish.

Serves 1

CURE-A-WHAT?

Curaçao—pronounced "cure-ah-so"—is named for the Dutch West Indian island in the Caribbean (itself named from the Spanish word *corazon,* meaning "heart"). It's a liqueur made with dried sour orange peel, a method popularized on that tiny island. The blue coloring just adds pizzazz; there's also green curaçao and, of course, clear or "white" curaçao.

'BAMA BREEZE

Blackberry hand pies and lemonade—that's Alabama in the summertime. This drink, which I like to serve in Mason jars, celebrates both treats. The added hint of orange makes it scrumptious.

1½ OUNCES BLACKBERRY LIQUEUR
1 OUNCE ORANGE LIQUEUR
½ OUNCE VODKA
½ CUP LEMONADE
Garnish: **BLACKBERRIES ON A SKEWER OR ORANGE CURL**

Pour all ingredients except the garnish into a cocktail shaker filled with ice; mix well.

Strain into a festive cocktail glass filled with ice. Add the garnish.

Serves 1

COLA HERBSAINT

It looks like murky Mississippi River water but tastes like a heaven filled with licorice. This simple-to-make but profoundly flavorful drink was a favorite of my grandmother's friend Thelma, who'd hold this old-time favorite in one hand, rattling the glass's ice, while stroking her chihuahua Tippy in the other. Tippy and I regarded each other warily. He'd often bare his teeth at me from afar—not growling, mind you, but just to look as threatening as a little dog can. Here's to holding your own, not matter what your lot in life.

2 OUNCES HERBSAINT OR PERNOD LIQUEUR
3 TO 4 OUNCES COCA-COLA
Garnish: **LICORICE OR PEPPERMINT STICK**

Pour the liqueur into a cocktail glass filled with cracked ice. Top with Coca-Cola. Add the garnish.

Serves 1

DERBY COOLER

Horse-racing fans often crave something a bit more gulpable than the bold and bourbony mint julep. Whether you're at a tailgating party at Churchill Downs or on your own deck with friends, a refreshing Derby Cooler is the winning ticket.

2 OUNCES BOURBON

1 OUNCE LIGHT RUM

2 OUNCES FRESHLY SQUEEZED ORANGE JUICE

1 OUNCE FRESHLY SQUEEZED LEMON JUICE

DASH OF GRENADINE

Garnish: **STAR FRUIT OR ORANGE SLICE**

Pour all ingredients except the garnish into a cocktail shaker filled with ice; mix vigorously.

Strain into 2 cocktail glasses filled with ice. Add the garnish.

Serves 2

WHO KNEW?

Daniel Boone's relative Wattie Boone was one of Kentucky's earliest distillers. He hired Abraham Lincoln's father, Thomas Lincoln, to work at his Boone's Nelson County distillery. Wattie predicted that young Abe was "bound to make a great man, no matter what trade he follows. If he goes into the whiskey business, he'll be the best distiller in the land."

Early Southerner George Washington had his own profitable whiskey distillery.

Bourbon is the only distilled spirit that increases in alcohol as it ages.

Alhough bourbon originated in Bourbon County in north central Kentucky, near Lexington, no whiskey is produced there now.

Kentucky makes 99 percent of all bourbon whiskey.

Many old bourbon barrels are sent to Scotland to help age Scotch.

Jack Daniel's is not classified as a "true" bourbon because it's charcoal-mellowed— filtered slowly through sugar-maple charcoal—before aging. This process gives it a unique character as it removes impurities. But other than the charcoal filtering, the Jack Daniel's production is very much like that of any other bourbon, and has just as much of a cult following. (See page 51 for more on Jack Daniel's.) George Dickel is another terrific Tennessee whiskey that can't technically be called a bourbon.

GUAVA MAMA

This is an addictive drink that I concocted one year in honor of Guavaween, the fall fund-raiser for Tampa's historic Latin district, Ybor City. Although it's a fund-raiser, the celebration is certainly no cakewalk. The naughty but nice event rivals New Orleans' Mardi Gras in attitude, as exemplified by the Mama Guava Stumble Parade's outrageous costumes and personalities. It's usually hot as hell, even in fall, and this drink is just the quencher, rum or no rum. Guava juice has a sweet, musky flavor.

2 OUNCES LIGHT RUM
3 OUNCES GUAVA NECTAR *(see Note)*
¾ OUNCE FRESHLY SQUEEZED LIME JUICE
1½ TEASPOONS SUPERFINE SUGAR
Garnish: **STAR FRUIT OR LIME SLICE**

Mix all ingredients except the garnish in a cocktail shaker filled with ice. Strain into a tall glass filled with ice. Add the garnish.

Serves 1

Note: Guava nectar can be found in the Hispanic food section of a grocery store or at a Hispanic market.

HIGH TEA

Long Island iced tea is anything but tea, which had me wondering: What would spiked sweet tea taste like? Fabulous, actually. This version uses lemon-flavored rum, but any fruity one would be fine. Enjoy it on its own, at a brunch, or with a plate of fried chicken, potato salad, and sliced ripe tomatoes.

2 OUNCES LEMON-INFUSED RUM
2 OUNCES CHILLED ICED TEA, SWEETENED
Garnish: **LEMON WEDGES**

Pour the rum and tea into a highball glass filled with ice and mix well. Add the garnish.

Serves 1

PEACH MOJITO

Judging by chichi bar menus, the Cuban mojito has come a long way from a sugarcane harvester's drink made of cane water, unrefined rum, and a handful of mint. By proximity, Floridians have long played with the drink, adding this tropical fruit or that. Here, the sprightly sensation is Georgia'd up with peach nectar and schnapps.

4 TO 6 FRESH MINT LEAVES

2 OUNCES PEACH NECTAR

1½ OUNCES LIGHT RUM

1 OUNCE PEACH SCHNAPPS

1½ OUNCES CLUB SODA

Garnishes: **PEACH SLICE OR LIME WEDGE, MINT SPRIG, AND SUGARCANE STICK**

Using a bar spoon, muddle the mint in the bottom of a tall Collins or pilsner glass. Fill with ice.

Add the nectar, rum, and schnapps to a cocktail shaker filled with ice; shake well.

Strain the mixture into the glass and top with club soda. Add the garnishes.

Serves 1

REFINED STRAWBERRY DAIQUIRI

Forget that brazenly hyper-sweet, hyper-red frozen stuff that comes from a machine and gets tarted up with canned whipped cream. Let's be more refined, shall we? When strawberries are plentiful and succulent, fresh is always best. This easy-to-make, pretty-in-pink recipe proves it.

1 POUND FRESH STRAWBERRIES *(16 to 18 berries)*
1 CUP LIGHT RUM
1 CUP POWDERED SUGAR
½ CUP *(4 ounces)* FRESHLY SQUEEZED LIME JUICE
Garnish: 4 STRAWBERRIES WITH LEAVES

Remove the hulls from the strawberries and add the berries to a blender. Pour in the rum, powdered sugar, and lime juice. Fill the container with the ice (about 2 cups; crushed ice is easier on your blender blades).

Process the mixture until well combined, adding more ice if desired.

For the garnish, slice the strawberries partway, from the bottom up, and place one on the rim of each of 4 wide-mouth cocktail glasses.

Serves 4

SCARLETT O'HARA

Like Miss Scarlett herself, this cocktail has an edge within its guise of scarlet-colored sweetness. And it would certainly be appreciated after finishing Margaret Mitchell's 1,037-page saga of Scarlett and Rhett and Ashley and the rest of the book's dysfunctional family. Atlanta's Miss Margaret (1900–1949) was quite the socialite, who listened intently to family friends tell stories of the war of Northern aggression. "When we went calling, I was usually scooped up onto a lap—told that I didn't look like a soul on either side of the family—and then forgotten for the rest of the afternoon while the gathering spiritedly refought the Civil War," she recalled. "Cavalry knees had the tendency to trot and bounce and jog in the midst of reminiscences and this kept me from going to sleep—fortunately for *Gone With the Wind*." Here's to being a good listener.

1½ OUNCES SOUTHERN COMFORT

1½ OUNCES CRANBERRY JUICE

½ OUNCE ROSE'S LIME JUICE, OR MORE TO TASTE *(see Note)*

Garnish: MARASCHINO CHERRY OR LIME WHEEL

Pour all ingredients except the garnish into a cocktail shaker filled with ice; mix well. Strain into an old-fashioned glass filled with ice or a chilled martini glass. Add the garnish.

Serves 1

Note: Rose's is sweetened Key lime juice; use it here instead of regular lime juice, which can be too tart.

SEE-THROUGH SANGRÍA

My family was never into drinking wine, and the complimentary sangría we were given at an over-the-top "Mexican" restaurant in Baton Rouge didn't help the situation. That deeply red, sickly sweet version always gave each of us a "second smile"—and quite the hangover. Needless to say, I've been delighted to discover more dignified recipes for the beverage. This is a white sangría I fell in love with while living in Texas, where the fruity wine spritzer, beautifully presented in a clear glass pitcher, offered relief from the heat of both the outdoors and authentic Mexican fare.

1 *(750-ml)* BOTTLE DRY WHITE WINE

½ CUP ORANGE LIQUEUR

¼ CUP SUGAR

1 UNPEELED LIME, THINLY SLICED *(remove the seeds)*

1 UNPEELED LEMON, THINLY SLICED *(remove the seeds)*

1 UNPEELED SMALL ORANGE, THINLY SLICED *(remove the seeds)*

1½ CUPS SLICED FRESH STRAWBERRIES

1½ CUPS HALVED GREEN GRAPES

2 CUPS CHILLED SPARKLING WATER OR CLUB SODA,
OR MORE TO TASTE

Garnish: WHOLE STRAWBERRIES WITH HULLS

Combine the wine, liqueur, sugar, and fruit in a large pitcher and refrigerate overnight. Pour into cocktail glasses filled with ice and top off with club soda. For the garnish, slice the strawberries partway, from the bottom up, and place one on the rim of each cocktail glass or wine goblet.

Serves 8 to 10

THE ULTIMATE MARGARITA

Friend Park Kerr, El Paso Chile Company founder and party host extraordinaire, calls this Southern favorite his "über-rita"—and he should know. He's tasted many a margarita in the quest to make and market the perfect tequila. Because of his commitment to authenticity, I prefer his company's Tequila Nacional, which incorporates agave plants from the Los Altos region of Jalisco (see sources, page 117). "Adding an extra citrus splash of fresh orange juice, or, equally great, pineapple juice, makes a margi come alive," Park says.

1 LIME WEDGE

KOSHER SALT ON A SMALL PLATE

1½ OUNCES PREMIUM SILVER TEQUILA

1 OUNCE COINTREAU LIQUEUR

1 OUNCE FRESHLY SQUEEZED LIME JUICE

ABOUT 1 TABLESPOON SUPERFINE SUGAR

1 TO 2 LIME WEDGES, PLUS MORE FOR GARNISH

Run the lime wedge around the rim of a margarita or cocktail glass. Dip the moistened rim in the salt. Set the lime wedge aside and chill the glass until ready to use.

Fill a cocktail shaker with about 1½ cups crushed ice and add the tequila, Cointreau, lime juice, and sugar. Shake vigorously to blend and chill.

Fill the prepared glass with ice cubes. Strain the shaken mixture into the glass. Squeeze 1 or 2 lime wedges into the drink, depending on personal preference. Drop the lime wedges into the drink and serve. Add more lime wedges to garnish.

Serves 1

WATERMELON CRUSH

Man oh man, the joy of summer is biting into a cold slice of watermelon. In this case, it's drinking that ice-cold fruit with a bit of rum. Offering the slush-fun in a pitcher's just fine, but I like to serve it in an old-fashioned pickle jar. I use Nannie's ladle to scoop it into glass canning jars garnished with a small wedge of watermelon. Try this with honeydew melon sometime.

8 CUPS SEEDED, CUBED WATERMELON *(about 4 pounds)*

1⅓ CUPS LIGHT RUM

**1½ CUPS FRESHLY SQUEEZED ORANGE JUICE,
OR MORE TO TASTE**

½ CUP ORANGE LIQUEUR

¼ CUP POWDERED SUGAR, OR MORE TO TASTE

2 OUNCES FRESHLY SQUEEZED LIME JUICE

Put the watermelon cubes in a plastic freezer bag; freeze for at least 8 hours.

Purée the watermelon and the remaining ingredients in batches in a blender or food processor until smooth, scraping down the sides occasionally. Combine the processed mixture well.

Serve in a large old pickle jar or a punch bowl and scoop the mixture into Mason jars, tin cups, or other festive glasses.

Serves 6

UPSY-DAISY LEMONADE

"Upsy-daisy" is what my grandmother would say when getting up from her chair after a cocktail jaunt. That's my thought exactly after messing around with this kicky drink. Here's your chance to use those little drink parasols you've been saving for whatever reason.

4 OUNCES FRESHLY SQUEEZED ORANGE JUICE

4 OUNCES SWEET AND SOUR MIX

4 OUNCES GOOD-QUALITY TEQUILA OR LIGHT RUM

4 OUNCES ORANGE LIQUEUR

2 CUPS LEMONADE OR LEMON-LIME DRINK

Garnishes: LEMON WHEEL, PARASOL

Combine the orange juice, sweet and sour, tequila, and liqueur in a medium container and let chill for several hours. Stir in the lemonade just before serving. Pour into tall cocktail glasses filled with ice. Add the garnishes.

Serves 4

Chapter Four: PINKIES UP

BRUNCHES, WEDDINGS, ANNIVERSARIES, GRADUATIONS, AND LUNCHEONS MAKE
BEAUTIFUL BACKDROPS FOR THESE PRIM AND PROPER SOUTHERN SIPPERS.

CHAMPAGNE PUNCH

This punch is as important to have at a wedding reception as it is to not wear white shoes after Labor Day. Southern women can make any number of variations of this in their sleep. A classic wedding or anniversary reception beverage, it is addictively refreshing—which is nice when you're all dolled up and fending off wilting humidity. During my early days in Mississippi, it was one of the few "proper" drinks that town matriarchs weren't ashamed of going back for repeatedly, requesting "just a wee bit more, thank you." Serving it in punch cups is the norm, but wineglasses are gaining in popularity.

1 CUP TRIPLE SEC

1 CUP COGNAC

½ CUP ORANGE LIQUEUR

2 CUPS UNSWEETENED PINEAPPLE JUICE

1 QUART CHILLED GINGER ALE

2 *(750-ml)* BOTTLES DRY CHAMPAGNE OR SPARKLING WINE, CHILLED

Garnishes: EDIBLE FLOWERS FOR CUPS,
PINEAPPLE SLICES FOR PUNCH BOWL

Combine the Triple Sec, cognac, orange liqueur, and pineapple juice in a large pitcher and stir well. Chill the mixture, covered, for several hours or overnight.

In a large punch bowl, combine the Triple Sec mixture, ginger ale, and champagne. Add ice cubes or crushed ice. Garnish as desired.

Serves 10 to 12

ABSINTHE FRAPPE

At the first cool sip on your fevered lip
You determine to live through the day
Life's again worthwhile as with a dawning smile
You imbibe your absinthe frappé.
— Victor Herbert, composer

This drink was popular with Parisian bohemians before it landed in the hands of their New Orleans brethren. Now this French Quarter cocktail is the height of old-style imbibing. Years ago, they made it with egg white, but I like this updated version better.

1½ OUNCES PERNOD OR HERBSAINT LIQUEUR
¾ OUNCE SIMPLE SYRUP *(page 22)*
2 OR 3 DASHES PEYCHAUD'S OR ANGOSTURA BITTERS
SPARKLING OR STILL WATER

Pour the liqueur, syrup, and bitters into a small cocktail glass filled with cracked ice. Add a splash of water.

Serves 1

THE BEE'S KNEES

Tampa friend Debbie Clifton Perez introduced me to this honey of a drink. It's like liquid gold, with honey and lemon—smooth and to the point. I can see why she fell in love with her husband, Fernando, over a round of these. The duo introduce the drink to others whenever they can. Though some use pure honey and stir it into the drink until it's completely dissolved, I've adapted it here to give it as much smoothness as possible. You can also make it with vodka, but the juniper berry base in the gin gives it more depth. I hear that in the '20s this drink was popular with the Lost Generation. I'm glad it's been rediscovered.

4 OUNCES GIN
1½ OUNCES HONEY SYRUP *(page 22)*
1 OUNCE FRESHLY SQUEEZED LEMON JUICE
Garnish: **LEMON CURLS** *(optional)*

Pour all ingredients except the garnish into a cocktail shaker filled with ice; shake well.

Strain into chilled cocktail or martini glasses. Add the garnish, if desired.

Serves 2

BLACKBERRY CORDIAL

Blackberries always remind me of the stained fingers I'd have after romping in a U-pick farm in Arkansas. We'd often stop there on the way back from Hot Springs, where we would enjoy a free time-share resort vacation orchestrated by my crafty mother (who changed our names slightly each year so they wouldn't catch on). I wasn't as interested in the time-share trips as I was in the resort's pool—and the ride home, when those ebonized treats were to be harvested. We'd baby those berries until they got home with us, where we'd use them for ice cream or pies. Now I baby the berries for this more adult tradition, one enjoyed for centuries in the South.

3 CUPS CRUSHED BLACKBERRIES *(about 1½ quarts whole berries)*

4 CUPS BRANDY

2 CUPS SIMPLE SYRUP *(page 22)*

Combine the berries with 3 cups of the brandy and steep for 1 week, stirring occasionally to release more of the berry flavor. Strain through cheesecloth into a clean container.

Add the remaining 1 cup brandy and the simple syrup. Store in the refrigerator for about a month before serving in cordial glasses.

Serves 10 to 12

CHIC COSMOPOLITAN

This very, um, "she-she" cosmopolitan hails from the Junior League of Tampa, a group of the most sophisticated and community-minded women you'll ever find. Junior League gals used to get a bad rap for their pearls and social-climbing prowess. Now they're revered for their pearls and power.

1 CUP CRANBERRY JUICE COCKTAIL

3 OUNCES VODKA

2 OUNCES GRAND MARNIER

½ OUNCE FRESHLY SQUEEZED LEMON JUICE

Combine all the ingredients in a cocktail shaker filled with ice; shake vigorously. Strain into chilled martini glasses.

Serves 2

MEMPHIS BELLE

This one's slightly sweet, with a wee bit of bite—just like a Memphis belle. It's said to be named for World War II's most famous B-17 bomber, the Flying Fortress, now on display in Memphis after having flown 25 combat missions over Europe. Speaking of battles, there are two versions of this drink floating around. Some bartenders use equal parts Southern Comfort and Baileys Irish Cream, but I prefer this sleeker version.

1½ OUNCES BRANDY

3 OR 4 DASHES ANGOSTURA OR ORANGE BITTERS

½ OUNCE FRESHLY SQUEEZED LEMON JUICE

¾ OUNCE SOUTHERN COMFORT

Garnish: LEMON TWIST

Add all ingredients except the garnish to a shaker filled with ice; shake well. Strain into a chilled martini or cocktail glass. Add the garnish.

Serves 1

EUPHORIC EGGNOG

I call this "euphoric" because it's euphorically easy to make, as well as delicious. You could make eggnog from scratch, and I would be most impressed, but who wants to be fussing with a boatload of eggs while you're trying to get ready for your party? (Plus, there's always a concern about some folks' ability to consume raw or slightly cooked eggs.) Just do as my grandmother did: Make "instanog," as I'd aggravatingly call it while she shushed me in our clothing store's kitchen. We served it this way for years and not a soul complained—they just got tipsy and bought lots of holiday pantsuits and dresses. Now, when I serve it, my friends take away their own find—the recipe.

10 SCOOPS (3½ CUPS) FRENCH VANILLA ICE CREAM,
PREFERABLY WITH VANILLA BEAN SEEDS

1½ CUPS PURCHASED EGGNOG

½ CUP BOURBON

½ CUP BRANDY

2 TO 3 TABLESPOONS ORANGE LIQUEUR *(optional)*

¼ TEASPOON GRATED NUTMEG

Garnishes: CHOCOLATE SHAVINGS OR FRESHLY GRATED NUTMEG

Combine all the ingredients except the garnishes in a blender; blend on the lowest speed until the mixture is smooth and frothy.

Pour into a pitcher and sprinkle with the garnish.

Serves 8 to 10

FIG PRESERVE MARTINI

I recently experienced a fig martini not in the Deep South, but deep in the heart of San Francisco's Russian Hill district, at a magnificent bar and eatery called Street. I began researching fig martini recipes online and couldn't find one—they tend to be well-guarded secrets. Well, fig fans, after much trial and error, I did it. Here's my creation that truly reflects a taste of the South: fig preserves. Just as in the preserves, ample orange overtones make it mesmerizing.

2 OUNCES FIG-INFUSED VODKA *(recipe follows)*
1½ OUNCES FRESHLY SQUEEZED ORANGE JUICE
Garnish: ORANGE CURL

Combine the vodka and orange juice in a cocktail shaker filled with ice. Shake until well combined. Strain into a chilled martini glass. Add garnish.

Serves 1

FIG-INFUSED VODKA

2 CUPS ORANGE JUICE OR WATER
1 POUND DRIED FIGS (PREFERABLY TURKISH OR CALIMYRNA), CHOPPED AND PITTED
2 CUPS VODKA

Bring the liquid to a boil and remove from the heat. Prick the figs with a fork and add to the liquid. Cover and let the figs plump in the hot liquid for about 10 minutes. Drain.

Let the figs steep in the vodka in a clean container for a week or two (the longer the better), shaking occasionally.

Using a fine-mesh strainer, coffee filter, or clean T-shirt, strain the infused vodka into a clean container, leaving the small seeds behind. Keep refrigerated for several months.

Makes about 2½ cups

HERBSAINT CHAMPAGNE COCKTAIL

Besides the French 75, this is another genteel way to enjoy champagne—with Herbsaint (liquid licorice, in essence). This sophisticated drink hails from one of New Orleans's absolute best restaurants, Herbsaint, named for the liqueur of local fame. There, bartender Monica Zeringue keeps patrons aglow with great drinks before, during, and after dinner.

⅛ TEASPOON *(3 or 4 drops)* HERBSAINT OR RICARD LIQUEUR
½ TEASPOON CRÈME DE MÛRE *(blackberry liqueur)*
CHAMPAGNE OR DRY SPARKLING WINE
Garnish: FRESH BLACKBERRY OR LEMON TWIST

Add the Herbsaint and crème de mûre to a champagne flute. Fill with champagne. Add the garnish.

Serves 1

ABSINTHE, ABSALOM!

After the first glass [of absinthe], you see things as you wish they were. After the second, you see things as they are not. Finally you see things as they really are, and that is the most horrible thing in the world.
— Oscar Wilde

Oh, the glory days of absinthe. In this country, that was pre-1912, before the green, anise-heavy liqueur was banned for allegedly driving people mad.

In its earliest form, absinthe—essentially wormwood leaves soaked in wine—derived from the Greek word *apsinthium*, meaning "undrinkable," because of its bitterness. It was appreciated for its medicinal properties.

Absinthe as we know it (or would like to have known it) derived from Pierre Ordinaire, a French doctor who invented the 136-proof healing tonic in 1792, using wormwood,

anise, and a host of wild herbs. The formula was handed down and refined over time until it wound up in the hands of Henri-Louis Pernod (sound familiar?).

Variations of absinthe made their way to New Orleans by 1837, when it was marketed as Herbsaint, Milky Way, and Green Opal. At the Old Absinthe House, absinthe frappes were sipped by a Who's Who of royalty, literary figures, and politicians. There, the green spirit was served the way it was in France—from brass faucets that slowly dripped cool water over sugar cubes placed on slotted spoons above the glasses. The bar's liqueur of choice, Legendre absinthe, reportedly morphed into Herbsaint (French for "holy herb"), which, along with the pastis liqueurs Pernod and Ricard, is the only available reinterpretation of the original (in this country, at least).

MEYER LEMONTINI

Meyer lemons have been cultivated for decades in the South, ever since "plant hunter" Frank N. Meyer first discovered the stunted citrus tree in China in 1908 and brought specimens back to grow in the United States. Their magic lies in their sweetness—they're much less tart than traditional lemons and are thought to be a cross between a lemon and a mandarin orange. Meyer lemons also tend to be small, with golden, thin-skinned rinds, making them very attractive as garnishes. These "gourmet" lemons are the current rage, showing up in desserts, lemonade, simple syrups, iced teas, and, here, cocktails. This simple martini beautifully embodies the flavor of summer.

2 OUNCES FRESHLY SQUEEZED MEYER LEMON JUICE *(see Note)*
¼ CUP SUPERFINE SUGAR
4 OUNCES VODKA
Garnish: **MEYER LEMON SLICES OR CURLS**

Rub the rims of 2 chilled martini glasses with a portion of the lemon used for the juice. Dip the rim of each glass in a plate of superfine sugar.

Add the vodka and Meyer lemon juice to a cocktail shaker filled with ice; mix vigorously.

Strain the mixture into the glasses. Add the garnish.

Serves 2

Note: If you can't find Meyer lemons locally, see the sources on page 117 for a good online purveyor.

SLOE GIN RICKEY

Ladies who lunch have been sipping this for decades throughout the Deep South, where the bright red, very sweet drink matches the flushed faces that usually follow the first glass. Sloe gin is made from sloes, the fruit of the wild blackthorn bush, which are steeped in gin. The resulting liquor is then aged in wooden barrels. Cassis adds a touch of black currant and is a slight twist popular in Natchez. This is certainly a togetherness drink, to be served in your finest crystal pitcher.

1 CUP SLOE GIN

2 OUNCES FRESHLY SQUEEZED LEMON JUICE

1½ CUPS SIMPLE SYRUP *(page 22)*

2½ CUPS SPARKLING WATER

6 DASHES CRÈME DE CASSIS

Garnishes: MINT SPRIGS AND LEMON WHEELS

Combine the sloe gin, lemon juice, syrup, and sparkling water in a pitcher and add cracked ice. Pour into wine goblets filled with cracked ice, and top each with a dash of cassis. Add the garnishes.

Serves 6

MINT JULEP MARTINI

They make martinis out of everything else; why not out of the lauded mint julep? A hint of vanilla makes this one unique. We like to serve this in pale red martini glasses at fall holiday parties, but on other occasions we opt for a more decorative glass. Its clear color belies its boldness.

7 FRESH MINT LEAVES
1 TABLESPOON SIMPLE SYRUP *(page 22)*
2 OUNCES VANILLA VODKA
Garnish: **SUGAR-COATED MINT SPRIG** *(see Note)*

Add the mint leaves and simple syrup to a cocktail shaker; muddle the mint to release flavor. Add the vodka and ice; shake until well combined. Strain into a chilled martini glass. Add the garnish.

Serves 1

Note: To coat mint in sugar, dip the sprig into a small dish of simple syrup before dredging it in superfine or granulated sugar.

PRALINE COFFEE

This is a trumped up version of café au lait (which, as a child, I thought was "café olé"). The butter smooths out the milk-laced coffee, and the liqueur gives it attitude. Since it's so sweet, I like to serve it in small espresso or demitasse cups after dinner; you'll have just enough for everyone to have a little cup, plus a shot more.

1½ CUPS HOT COFFEE

⅓ CUP HALF-AND-HALF

1 TABLESPOON BUTTER

1 CUP PRALINE LIQUEUR

Garnish: **CINNAMON STICKS**

Combine the coffee, half-and-half, and butter in a small saucepan until thoroughly combined and the butter has melted. Add the praline liqueur just before pouring into espresso or demitasse cups. Add the garnish.

Serves 4 to 6

Chapter Five: NIBBLES

BE A RESPONSIBLE PARTY HOST: DON'T LET YOUR GUESTS DRINK ON AN EMPTY STOMACH. THESE EASY-TO-MAKE AND -EAT TREATS WILL BE PLEASANT DIVERSIONS.

PORK RINDS, *see page 116, Appetizers*

BEER-BATTERED STRING BEANS
with RIGHTEOUS RÉMOULADE SAUCE

This is a Southern twist on the parchment paper–lined cups of French fries so popular these days. The feather-light beer batter gives the mild-mannered green beans more definition (while still letting their color peek through), and the rémoulade sauce ramps up the flavor and balances cool with hot.

1 POUND GREEN BEANS

1 CUP BEER *(not dark)*

1 TEASPOON SALT

JUICE OF 1 LIME

1 CUP ALL-PURPOSE FLOUR

4 CUPS VEGETABLE OIL

RIGHTEOUS RÉMOULADE SAUCE *(page 99)*

2 LIMES, CUT INTO WEDGES, FOR SERVING

Clip off and discard the stalk ends of the green beans; set aside.

In a large bowl, whisk the beer, salt, and lime juice into the flour until smooth. (The mixture will foam slightly.)

Dredge the beans in the batter to coat.

In a deep skillet, heat the oil to 375 degrees F.

Working in batches, gently place about 10 battered beans into the hot oil and let cook for about 1 minute. Using a slotted spoon, transfer the fried beans to a paper bag or paper towel–lined plate to drain and cool. Repeat the process until the remaining beans are cooked.

Serve with Righteous Rémoulade Sauce and lime wedges.

Serves 4 to 6

Continued on next page

BEER-BATTERED STRING BEANS
with RIGHTEOUS RÉMOULADE SAUCE

Continued from previous page

RIGHTEOUS RÉMOULADE SAUCE

1 CUP MAYONNAISE

2 TABLESPOONS CREOLE OR WHOLE-GRAIN MUSTARD

2 TABLESPOONS KETCHUP

½ CUP FINELY CHOPPED GREEN ONIONS

2 TABLESPOONS FINELY CHOPPED FRESH PARSLEY

2 TABLESPOONS FINELY CHOPPED CELERY

2 CLOVES GARLIC, MINCED

1 TEASPOON PREPARED HORSERADISH SAUCE

1 TEASPOON PAPRIKA

1 TEASPOON HOT SAUCE

Whisk together all ingredients in a medium bowl. Cover and chill for 1 hour. Serve with Beer-Battered String Beans.

Makes 1⅔ cups

BLACK-EYED PEAS CON QUESO

Here we elevate the status of canned black-eyed peas. Instead of being a modest side dish, it's the main event, jazzed up with jalapeños, cilantro, and gooey hot cheese. Seriously: Be prepared to hand out this recipe just after you serve this dish—your friends will hound you otherwise.

¼ CUP (½ STICK) BUTTER OR MARGARINE

1 MEDIUM ONION, FINELY CHOPPED

2 CLOVES GARLIC, PRESSED

1 *(16-ounce)* LOAF PROCESSED CHEESE SPREAD, CUBED

1 TABLESPOON FINELY CHOPPED FRESH CILANTRO,
PLUS MORE FOR ADDED FLAVOR AND GARNISH

4 JALAPEÑO PEPPERS, SEEDED AND CHOPPED

2 *(15.8-ounce)* CANS BLACK-EYED PEAS, DRAINED

TORTILLA CHIPS, FOR SERVING

Melt the butter in a large Dutch oven. Add the onion and garlic and sauté until tender.

Add the cheese and cook over medium heat, stirring until melted.

Stir in the 1 tablespoon cilantro, peppers, and black-eyed peas. Reduce the heat and let the mixture simmer for 3 to 5 minutes or until thoroughly heated.

Transfer the dip to a serving dish (unless you're using a decorative Dutch oven). Sprinkle more chopped cilantro over the top.

Serve with tortilla chips.

Serves 6

COUNTRY HAM AND GOAT CHEESE PINWHEELS

Nannie and Mama stocked up on crescent rolls like they did on Oil of Olay. We always had roll-out dough and country ham in the refrigerator, and that was a good thing when it came to a quick baked lunch. In this case, the duo gets rolled into a super-quick appetizer updated with goat cheese, a variation on that third element of the refrigerator-staple trinity—cream cheese.

1 *(8-ounce)* CAN REFRIGERATED CRESCENT DINNER ROLLS

8 OUNCES THINLY SLICED COUNTRY HAM OR PROSCIUTTO

4 OUNCES SOFT GOAT CHEESE

½ TEASPOON FRESHLY GROUND BLACK PEPPER

1 TABLESPOON OLIVE OIL, PLUS MORE IF NEEDED

⅓ CUP CHOPPED FRESH BASIL

Preheat the oven to 375 degrees F. Spray 2 cookie sheets with cooking spray.

Separate the dinner roll dough into 4 rectangles on a lightly floured surface. Firmly press the perforations to seal them together.

Arrange the ham slices evenly over the rectangles.

In a small bowl, combine the cheese, pepper, and 1 tablespoon oil (adding more oil if necessary to further soften the cheese). Spread evenly over the ham on each rectangle. Sprinkle evenly with the basil.

Starting at the short end of a rectangle, roll it up, pressing the seams if they separate. Repeat with the remaining rectangles.

With serrated knife, cut each roll into 6 slices. Place on the cookie sheets, about 1 inch apart.

Bake for 15 to 20 minutes or until golden brown. Serve warm.

Serves 8 to 10 (makes 24 appetizers)

CRAB LOUIS COCKTAIL

What could be better with champagne (especially a French 75) than another "cocktail"? This dish reminds me a bit of dining at New Orleans' Galatoire's as a child, enjoying their Crabmeat Maison cocktail and seeing crisp white everywhere—from the tablecloths to the waiters' jackets to the fresh fish being set in front of me. This more delicate sauce, which my grandmother adored with fried fish, has a milder flavor than most rémoulades (and than Galatoire's sauce, which included capers and Creole mustard). Its mildness keeps it from overpowering the delicate fresh flavor of the crab. Jumbo lump crabmeat may be sold by the karat, but the white gems are worth every extra penny.

3 CUPS SHREDDED ICEBERG LETTUCE

2 TABLESPOONS LOUIS SAUCE *(page 105)*

1 POUND JUMBO LUMP CRABMEAT, BITS OF SHELL REMOVED

¼ TEASPOON KOSHER SALT *(optional)*

⅛ TEASPOON FRESHLY GROUND BLACK PEPPER *(optional)*

GRATED LEMON ZEST, FOR ADDED FLAVOR AND GARNISH

Place some shredded lettuce into each of 4 cocktail or martini glasses. Top with the Louis Sauce. Arrange equal portions of crabmeat on top. Season with salt and pepper, if desired. Sprinkle with lemon zest. Serve with additional sauce, if desired.

Serves 4

Continued on next page

CRAB LOUIS COCKTAIL

Continued from previous page

LOUIS SAUCE

Whipping cream makes this sauce fluffy, but if you're in a pinch, substitute 1 cup of mayonnaise.

1 *(12-ounce)* JAR CHILI SAUCE

1 CUP MAYONNAISE

1 CUP HEAVY WHIPPING CREAM, WHIPPED

2 TABLESPOONS GRATED ONION

½ TEASPOON GRATED LEMON ZEST

2 TEASPOONS FRESHLY SQUEEZED LEMON JUICE

1 TABLESPOON PREPARED HORSERADISH

1½ TEASPOONS CREOLE OR GREEK SEASONING

1 TEASPOON WORCESTERSHIRE SAUCE

1 TEASPOON HOT SAUCE

Combine all of the ingredients in a medium bowl, stirring well. Cover and refrigerate until ready to serve in Crab Louis Cocktail.

Makes 3 cups

Note: Leftover Louis Sauce is excellent with quesadillas.

DEVILISH EGGS

Everyone loves deviled eggs as one-bite salads before Sunday lunch, but let's enjoy them after-hours too. This hipper, spicier version of its no-frills cousin has a Tex-Mex touch for a bit of mischief (I enjoyed similar eggs at barbecues when I lived in Austin). The smokiness derives from the chipotle chiles—brick-colored dried jalapeños—that give punch to the thick and vinegary adobo sauce.

12 LARGE HARD-BOILED EGGS, PEELED

1/3 CUP SOUR CREAM

1/4 CUP MAYONNAISE

1 1/2 TABLESPOONS GRATED ONION

2 TEASPOONS FINELY CHOPPED FRESH CILANTRO

2 TEASPOONS CHOPPED CHIPOTLE CHILE IN ADOBO SAUCE
(about 1 chile; see Note)

2 TEASPOONS ADOBO SAUCE FROM THE CHILES

1/2 TEASPOON SALT

Garnish: **FRESH CILANTRO LEAVES AND PAPRIKA** *(optional)*

Halve the eggs, placing the hard-cooked yolks in a small bowl. Using a fork, mash the yolks until smooth. Stir in the sour cream, mayonnaise, onion, cilantro, chipotle, adobo sauce, and salt.

Using a spoon or pastry bag, add the stuffing mixture to the egg halves. Garnish with cilantro leaves and paprika, if desired. Store in the refrigerator for several hours or overnight before serving.

Serves 8 to 10

Note: Chipotle chiles are found in the Hispanic food section of most grocery stores.

FEISTY VIDALIA ONION CHEESE TOASTS

I smile to myself every time I hear about Vidalia onions. For years I thought they sprang from the earth of Vidalia, Louisiana, just across the Mississippi River from Natchez, and I took great pride in that. It wasn't until I got out of college that I became aware of Vidalia, Georgia—and its claim to fame. Oh well. Either way, these yellow-skinned globes of white remind me of spring and, more so, of cooking with Nannie, who could be found sautéing them on the Thermador range my mother won on the game show *The Price Is Right* during a trip to New York City, where she got her hair fixed by a celebrity stylist. But I digress.

24 SLICES FRENCH BAGUETTE OR HEARTY BREAD SLICES, ½ INCH THICK

1 TABLESPOON BUTTER

1¾ CUPS FINELY CHOPPED VIDALIA OR SWEET ONIONS

1 ¾ CUPS GRATED MOZZARELLA CHEESE

3 JALAPEÑO PEPPERS, SEEDED AND CHOPPED

2 MEDIUM TOMATOES, CHOPPED AND DRAINED

1 CUP MAYONNAISE

1 TEASPOON CAYENNE PEPPER

½ TEASPOON SALT, OR TO TASTE

FRESHLY GROUND PEPPER, TO TASTE

Arrange the bread slices on a baking sheet and toast until lightly browned; set aside.

Melt the butter in a medium skillet. Add the onions and stir until softened. Set aside to cool slightly.

Preheat the broiler.

In a medium bowl, combine the remaining ingredients, folding in the onions.

Spread the cheese mixture on top of the bread slices, leaving some room for the cheese to melt to the edges. Broil for 4 to 5 minutes, until melted and lightly browned.

Serves 8 to 10

FREDDIE LEE'S CHEESE PENNIES

These little cheese crackers are "so light you have to hold 'em so they won't float away," my mom, Freddie Lee, would say about her recipe for the Southern cocktail-hour standard. The secret here is the sifted flour, which makes them lighter in texture. Despite the longstanding name, the "penny" size isn't as fun to eat as the quarter size. You can freeze the dough (wrapped in aluminum foil) until you're ready to slice and bake it.

½ CUP *(1 stick)* UNSALTED BUTTER, AT ROOM TEMPERATURE

2½ CUPS GRATED SHARP CHEDDAR CHEESE

½ TEASPOON WORCESTERSHIRE SAUCE

½ TEASPOON HOT SAUCE, OR MORE TO TASTE

1 CUP ALL-PURPOSE FLOUR, SIFTED

PECAN HALVES *(optional)*

Cream the butter, using a fork. Mix in the cheese and sauces; stir to blend.

Slowly stir in the flour until just blended. Turn the dough out onto a lightly floured surface and shape into a roll. Cover in plastic wrap and chill for several hours.

When chilled, slice the dough into 2 pieces. Roll each section into a log shaped like a long breadstick measuring about 1 inch thick.

Preheat the oven to 350 degrees F.

Slice each dough section into ¼-inch-thick "coins" and place on a lightly greased cookie sheet. If desired, press pecan halves into them, or, better yet, leftover Sweet and Sassy Pecans (page 114).

Bake for 10 to 15 minutes or until golden brown and lightly crisp.

Makes about 5 dozen

Note: Store leftover pennies in an airtight container. When working with frozen dough, thaw, then bake for 10 to 15 minutes at 350 degrees F.

SHRIMP IN STOLES
WITH DR PEP BBQ SAUCE

Nannie and I would laugh that one of her old Cajun cookbooks called fried shrimp "shrimp in pants." A similar take on shrimp is at play in this recipe for bacon-wrapped shrimp. It's fabulous with a Dr Pepper–based barbecue sauce, which was my secret recipe until now.

20 THICK, ROUND WOODEN PICKS OR SKEWERS

20 LARGE, FRESH SHRIMP, PEELED AND DEVEINED

2 TABLESPOONS OLIVE OIL

1 CUP FRESHLY SQUEEZED ORANGE JUICE

1 TEASPOON PRESSED FRESH GINGER *(use a garlic press)*

¼ TEASPOON SALT

⅛ TEASPOON FRESHLY GROUND BLACK PEPPER

20 SLICES PRECOOKED BACON *(see Note)*

DR PEP BBQ SAUCE *(page 112)*

Soak the picks in water for 30 minutes (so they won't burn on the grill).

Combine the shrimp, olive oil, orange juice, ginger, salt, and pepper in a mixing bowl; marinate for 20 to 30 minutes (any longer than that and the shrimp may toughen).

Heat the grill to medium-high heat (350 degrees F).

Wrap 1 bacon slice around each shrimp and secure with a pick.

Grill the bacon-wrapped shrimp for about 6 minutes or until the shrimp turn pink, turning once.

Serve with Dr Pep BBQ Sauce.

Serves 5 to 6

Continued on next page

Note: For ease, I like to use the ready-to-heat, precooked bacon; it always grills to a crisp (which is a nice change of pace from the soggy wraps we sometimes end up with). If you choose to start with raw bacon, use 10 slices and cut them in half; microwave in batches for about 2 minutes and let cool before wrapping around each shrimp.

SHRIMP IN STOLES
WITH DR PEP BBQ SAUCE

Continued from previous page

DR PEP BBQ SAUCE

The Dr Pepper soft drink popped up in 1885—one year before Coca-Cola—in Waco, Texas (formerly known as Six Shooter Junction—I kid you not). It was in Wade Morrison's Old Corner Drug Store, where a pharmacist combined a unique mix of spices into what we get a kick out of drinking today. This sauce, which has endless depth of flavor, is also fabulous on ribs and chicken and brisket and sausage and pork and . . . make me stop.

3 TABLESPOONS FRESHLY SQUEEZED LEMON JUICE

1 CLOVE GARLIC, PRESSED

1 TEASPOON PRESSED FRESH GINGER *(use a garlic press)*

1 SLICE SWEET ONION, ½ INCH THICK

1 CUP CHERRY VANILLA–FLAVORED DR PEPPER *(see Note)*

1½ CUPS KETCHUP

3 TABLESPOONS WORCESTERSHIRE SAUCE

2 TEASPOONS HOT SAUCE

1 TABLESPOON CIDER VINEGAR

SEA SALT, TO TASTE

Combine all of the ingredients in a heavy, nonreactive saucepan and slowly bring to a boil over medium heat.

Reduce the heat and let the sauce simmer until thick and the flavors have melded, about 20 minutes. Adjust the seasonings to your liking.

Strain the sauce into a bowl and let cool to room temperature. Refrigerate, covered, and serve with Shrimp in Stoles.

Makes about 2 cups

Note: Cherry vanilla–flavored Dr Pepper boosts the sauce's flavor, but if you can't find it, go with the standard version.

SPIKED PIMIENTO CHEESE

As Elvis might say, "A little less conversation, a little more action." That's what this jalapeño-charged cheese spread is all about. We, like many across the South, keep it in the fridge for our own snacking, as well as for friends to have with their cocktails. It's fun to serve it on little bread slices, celery sticks, or crisp crackers. My family always liked it drier to help bring out the color and flavor of the cheese; the real mayonnaisey kind reminded us too much of the plastic container variety at the A&P.

1¼ CUPS MAYONNAISE, OR MORE TO TASTE

1 *(4-ounce)* JAR DICED PIMIENTO, DRAINED

2 TO 3 JALAPEÑO PEPPERS, SEEDED AND FINELY CHOPPED

1 TEASPOON WORCESTERSHIRE SAUCE

2 TEASPOONS FINELY GRATED ONION

¼ TEASPOON CAYENNE PEPPER

1 *(8-ounce)* BLOCK EXTRA-SHARP CHEDDAR CHEESE, FINELY GRATED

1 *(8-ounce)* BLOCK SHARP YELLOW OR WHITE CHEDDAR CHEESE, GRATED

Garnish: PAPRIKA *(for subtle flavor and color)* OR CAYENNE PEPPER *(for more heat, if you're game)*

Combine the mayonnaise, pimiento, peppers, Worcestershire, onion, and cayenne in a large mixing bowl. Gently fold in the cheeses and refrigerate before serving. Sprinkle with paprika or cayenne.

Makes 4 cups, serving 14 to 16

SWEET AND SASSY PECANS

Many Southerners might as well put "pecan sommelier" on their résumés, since hordes of us like to seek out and savor the many pecan textures and flavors affiliated with our regions. Because the earthy nut is so plentiful, we find ourselves dressing them up in a host of ways— sometimes fiery, sometimes sweet. In this case, they're both. My brother Dempse is a master at making pecans that sizzle.

⅓ CUP SUGAR

¼ CUP *(½ stick)* BUTTER

¼ CUP ORANGE JUICE

2 TEASPOONS CREOLE OR CAJUN SEASONING

½ TO 1 TEASPOON CAYENNE PEPPER

4 CUPS *(about 1 pound)* PECAN HALVES

Preheat the oven to 250 degrees F.

Combine the sugar, butter, orange juice, Creole seasoning, and cayenne in a heavy skillet over medium heat, stirring until the butter melts and the sugar dissolves. Remove the skillet from the heat; add the nuts and toss to coat.

Place the coated pecan mixture in a single layer in an aluminum foil–lined 15-by-10-inch baking pan.

Bake for 1 hour, stirring every 15 minutes. Cool in the pan on a wire rack, separating the pecans with a fork. Store in an airtight container for up to 1 week, or freeze for up to 1 month.

Serves 8 to 10

Friends coming over and you're not remotely prepared? Isn't that always the case? Try these drinks and appetizers that can be ready in 5 minutes or less, using many things you already have at home or can pick up at the quickie mart.

APPETIZERS

Pork rinds (especially fun served in your finest silver bowl; your low-carb-dieting friends will love you).

Sweet potato chips.

Any combination of olives.

Pour hot pepper jelly or Pickapeppa sauce over a block of cream cheese; serve with crackers or toasted baguette slices.

Mix 1 tablespoon Creole, Cajun, or Greek seasoning into 1 cup of sour cream; adjust the seasoning to taste. Serve with thick-cut potato chips.

Pickled asparagus, green beans, and/or okra.

Spread refried beans or bean dip on tortilla chips, top with grated cheese, and microwave for 20 seconds. Top with salsa and/or sour cream.

Boiled peanuts.

DRINKS

MIMOSA: Mix equal parts fresh orange juice and champagne; serve in champagne flutes.

CUBA LIBRE: Pour 2 ounces rum into a highball glass filled with ice. Top with Coca-Cola and garnish with lime wedges.

SCREWDRIVER: Pour 1½ ounces vodka into a cocktail glass filled with ice. Top with fresh orange juice and garnish with an orange wheel.

GIN AND TONIC: Pour 1½ ounces gin into a cocktail glass filled with ice. Top with tonic and garnish with a lemon or lime wedge.

GIN CHILL: Pour 1½ ounces gin into a highball glass filled with ice. Top with ginger ale; garnish with a lime wedge.

SEA BREEZE: Pour 1½ ounces vodka into a cocktail glass filled with ice. Add 3 to 4 ounces grapefruit juice and 1 ounce cranberry juice. Garnish with a lime wedge.

CAPE COD: Pour 1½ ounces vodka into a cocktail glass filled with ice. Top with cranberry juice. Garnish with a lime wedge.

SOURCES

You Can Always Get What You Want

Some gourmet grocers and well-stocked liquor shops carry or can order the items that follow; call ahead to save on shipping fees.

FEE BROTHERS
www.feebrothers.com or
(800) 961-3337
Cocktail mixes, bitters, and flavoring syrups

INTERNET WINE AND SPIRITS
www.internetwines.com or
(877) 624-1982
Maraschino cherry liqueur, Pernod liqueur, Ricard liqueur

MARTIN WINE CELLAR
www.martinwine.com or
(888) 407-7496
Wines, spirits, flower water

MELISSA'S WORLD VARIETY PRODUCE
www.melissas.com or (800) 588-0151
Organic and exotic fruits; Meyer lemons; sugarcane swizzle sticks

SAZERAC COMPANY, INC.
www.sazerac.com or (504) 831-9450
Herbsaint liqueur, Peychaud's aromatic cocktail bitters, praline liqueur

SONOMA SYRUP CO.
www.sonomasyrup.com or
(707) 996-4070
Simple syrups and pure vanilla

TEQUILA NACIONAL
www.tequilanacional.com or
(915) 544-3434
Tequila, salsas, and dips

PERMISSIONS

Letter on pages 29–30 used with permission from author Robert L. Wolke.

The recipe for the Ultimate Margarita on page 68 is used with permission from *Viva Margarita* by W. Park Kerr (Chronicle Books, 2003).

The recipe for the Chic Cosmopolitan on page 82 is used with permission from *The Life of the Party* by the Junior League of Tampa (Favorite Recipes Press, 2003).

INDEX

ABSINTHE, 89

ABSINTHE FRAPPE, 76

ACCESSORIES, 17–19

APPETIZERS, 97–116

APPLE JOUJOU, 53

BAMA BREEZE, 56

THE BEE'S KNEES, 79

BLACKBERRY CORDIAL, 80

BLACKBERRY LIQUEUR
  'Bama Breeze, 56

BLACK-EYED PEAS CON QUESO, 100

BLOODY MARY, CREOLE, 34

BLUEBERRY MARTINI, 54

BOURBON, 33, 59
  Classic Mint Julep, 33
  The Crusta, 36
  Derby Cooler, 59
  Euphoric Eggnog, 84
  Milk Punch, 41
  The Sazerac, 47
  The Vieux Carré, 50

BRANDY
  Blackberry Cordial, 80
  Euphoric Eggnog, 84
  French 75, 38
  Memphis Belle, 83
  Milk Punch, 41

CAPE COD, 116

CHAMPAGNE
  Champagne Punch, 75
  French 75, 38
  Herbsaint Champagne Cocktail, 89
  Mimosa, 116

CHEESE
  Black-Eyed Peas con Queso, 100
  Country Ham and Goat Cheese
    Pinwheels, 102
  Feisty Vidalia Onion Cheese Toasts, 107
  Freddie Lee's Cheese Pennies, 108
  Spiked Pimiento Cheese, 113

CHIC COSMOPOLITAN, 82

COFFEE, PRALINE, 94

COGNAC
  Champagne Punch, 75
  The Crusta, 36
  The Roffignac, 49
  The Vieux Carré, 50

COLA-HERBSAINT, 57

COSMOPOLITAN, CHIC, 82

CRAB LOUIS COCKTAIL, 103

CREOLE BLOODY MARY, 34

THE CRUSTA, 36

CUBA LIBRE, 116

CURAÇAO, 54

DAIQUIRI, REFINED STRAWBERRY, 64

DERBY COOLER, 59

DR PEP BBQ SAUCE, 112

EGGNOG, EUPHORIC, 84

EGGS, DEVILISH, 106

FIG-INFUSED VODKA, 87

FIG PRESERVE MARTINI, 87

FLAVOR BOOSTERS, 25–26

FRENCH 75, 38

GARNISHES, 23–25

GEORGE DICKEL, 59

GIN
  The Bee's Knees, 79
  French 75, 38
  Gin and Tonic, 116
  Gin Chill, 116
  Orange Blossom, 42
  Ramos Gin Fizz, 46

GLASSES, 23

GUAVA MAMA, 60

HAM, COUNTRY, AND GOAT CHEESE
  PINWHEELS, 102

HERBSAINT, 89
  Absinthe Frappe, 76
  Cola Herbsaint, 57
  Herbsaint Champagne Cocktail, 89

HIGH TEA, 61

HONEY SYRUP, 22–23

THE HURRICANE, 37

JACK DANIEL'S, 51, 59

LEMONADE, UPSY-DAISY, 72
LIQUOR AND LIQUEUR CHECKLIST, 19–20
LOUIS SAUCE, 105

MARGARITA, THE ULTIMATE, 68
MEMPHIS BELLE, 83
MEYER LEMONTINI, 90
MILK PUNCH, 41
MIMOSA, 116
MINT JULEP, CLASSIC, 33
MINT JULEP MARTINI, 92
MINT SYRUP, 22
MOJITO, PEACH, 62

ONION CHEESE TOASTS, FEISTY VIDALIA, 107
ORANGE BLOSSOM, 42

PEACH MOJITO, 62
PECANS, SWEET AND SASSY, 114
PERNOD
    Absinthe Frappe, 76
    Cola Herbsaint, 57
PIMM'S CUP, 44
PLANTER'S PUNCH, 43
PRALINE COFFEE, 94

RAMOS GIN FIZZ, 46
RÉMOULADE SAUCE, RIGHTEOUS, 99
THE ROFFIGNAC, 49
RUM
    Cuba Libre, 116
    Derby Cooler, 59
    Guava Mama, 60
    High Tea, 61
    The Hurricane, 37
    Peach Mojito, 62
    Planter's Punch, 43
    Refined Strawberry Daiquiri, 64
    Upsy-Daisy Lemonade, 72
    Watermelon Crush, 71
RYE WHISKEY
    The Roffignac, 49
    The Sazerac, 47
    The Vieux Carré, 50

SANGRÍA, SEE-THROUGH, 67
THE SAZERAC, 47
SCARLETT O'HARA, 65
SCREWDRIVER, 116
SEA BREEZE, 116
SEE-THROUGH SANGRÍA, 67
SHRIMP IN STOLES, 111
SIMPLE SYRUP, 22
SLOE GIN RICKEY, 91
SOUTHERN COMFORT, 53
    Apple Joujou, 53
    Memphis Belle, 83
    Scarlett O'Hara, 65
STRAWBERRY DAIQUIRI, REFINED, 64
STRING BEANS, BEER-BATTERED, 97
SYRUPS, 22–23

TEA, HIGH, 61
TENNESSEE WHISKEY, 19, 51, 59
TEQUILA
    The Ultimate Margarita, 68
    Upsy-Daisy Lemonade, 72
TOASTS, 26–27

THE ULTIMATE MARGARITA, 68
UPSY-DAISY LEMONADE, 72

THE VIEUX CARRÉ, 50
VODKA
    'Bama Breeze, 56
    Blueberry Martini, 54
    Cape Cod, 116
    Chic Cosmopolitan, 82
    Creole Bloody Mary, 34
    Fig-Infused Vodka, 87
    Fig Preserve Martini, 87
    Meyer Lemontini, 90
    Mint Julep Martini, 92
    Screwdriver, 116
    Sea Breeze, 116

WATERMELON CRUSH, 71
WHISKEY. See BOURBON; RYE WHISKEY;
    TENNESSEE WHISKEY
WINE. See also CHAMPAGNE
    See-Through Sangría, 67

TABLE OF EQUIVALENTS

The exact equivalents in the following tables have been rounded for convenience.

LIQUID / DRY MEASURES

U.S.	METRIC
Dash	
¼ ounce	2 ml
Bar spoon	
½ ounce	15 ml
¼ teaspoon	1.25 milliliters
½ teaspoon	2.5 milliliters
1 teaspoon	5 milliliters
1 tablespoon (3 teaspoons)	15 milliliters
2 tablespoons (pony)	
1 fluid ounce	30 ml
3 tablespoons (jigger)	
1½ fluid ounces	45 ml
¼ cup	60 milliliters
⅓ cup	80 milliliters
½ cup	120 milliliters
1 cup	240 milliliters
1 pint (2 cups)	480 milliliters
1 quart (4 cups, 32 ounces)	960 milliliters
1 gallon (4 quarts)	3.84 liters
1 medium lemon equals	3 tablespoons juice
1 medium lime equals	1½ to 2 tablespoons juice
1 medium orange equals	⅓ cup juice
1 ounce (by weight)	28 grams
1 pound	448 grams
2.2 pounds	1 kilogram

LENGTH

U.S.	METRIC
⅛ inch	3 millimeters
¼ inch	6 millimeters
½ inch	12 millimeters
1 inch	2.5 centimeters

OVEN TEMPERATURE

FAHRENHEIT	CELSIUS	GAS
250	120	½
275	140	1
300	150	2
325	160	3
350	180	4
375	190	5
400	200	6
425	220	7
450	230	8
475	240	9
500	260	10